FINISHING WELL

Ian Knox qualified as a solicitor in 1966 at the age of 22, was National Evangelist with the Covenanters from 1970 to 1973, returned to the law and finally became a senior solicitor with Coventry City Council before joining the Church Pastoral Aid Society in 1982. He became Director of the 40:3 Trust in 1986, engaging in evangelism and teaching throughout the British Isles and across Africa until his retirement in 2009. He was made a canon of Webuye Cathedral in the diocese of Bungoma, Western Kenya, in 1999 and ordained priest there in the Anglican Church in 2005. He continues an active preaching ministry across Africa and in England. In January 2020, Ian Knox was made Canon Missioner at All Saints Cathedral, Boroboro, Diocese of Lango, Uganda. He is a successful author, whose books include *Bereaved, Older People in the Church, 50 Ways to Share Your Faith* and *100 Instant Faith-Sharing Talks*.

Ian has been married to Ruth for over 40 years. They have four sons and ten grandchildren. They currently live in rural Northumberland.

'Ian Knox has written a book about ageing that is full of wisdom and wit, from a global perspective, and redolent with Scripture. Thankfully, most of us will grow old (the alternative, as Ian notes, is to die young), and this book helps us approach that with hope and courage and purpose. He also writes as one who is arriving there himself, and so is mercifully short on glib responses to the challenges that come with the final stages of life.'
Revd Dr Paul Goodliff, General Secretary, Churches Together in England

'Christian churches, people and charities are conspicuously active in working with older people. Accessible to leaders and doers, this book is a vital call to set this activity in the biblical context of older age so that it can be of eternal significance.'
Stephen Hammersley, Chief Executive, Pilgrims' Friend Society

'For some, this book could prove to be lifechanging. Ian Knox has provided us with both an encouraging and challenging manuscript for those exploring one of the big questions of life, "How do I finish well?"'
Steve Clifford, former General Director, Evangelical Alliance

'Ian Knox's wealth of wisdom, experience and research are all encapsulated in this book. In reaching out to those in later life, we touch God's heart and so does this book. It deserves to be read by every Christian.'
Terry Puttick, Field Director, London City Mission

'*Finishing Well* is an excellent read – enjoyable, accessible and comforting, with the constant reminder of what the Bible says about older age and the plans God has for His people. As we are reminded of how God sees later life, we have so much to gain in our own lives as well as our churches and wider communities. This book will both inform and engage, and I commend it to you.'

Carl Knightly, Chief Executive, Faith in Later Life

FINISHING WELL

A God's-Eye View of Ageing

Ian Knox

First published in Great Britain in 2020

Society for Promoting Christian Knowledge
36 Causton Street
London SW1P 4ST
www.spck.org.uk

British Library Cataloguing-in-Publication Data
A catalogue record for this book is available from the British Library

ISBN 978–0-281-08349-7
eBook ISBN 978-0-281-08350-3

1 3 5 7 9 10 8 6 4 2

Typeset by Nord Compo
First printed in Great Britain by Jellyfish Print Solutions

eBook by Nord Compo

Produced on paper from sustainable forests

For

Joshua, Amelia, Elisabeth, Joshua, Joseph, Emily,
Samuel, Daniel, Elijah and Tobias,
who honour me with the name 'Grandpa'

Contents

Acknowledgments

This has been a book that could not have been written without the generosity of many. Thank you to all who have helped:

- Garry Williams, Stephen Hammersley and David Field, for getting me to read a ridiculous number of books! But also for your encouragement, advice and wise counsel.
- Roger Hitchings, for allowing me to use his notes in Chapter 6.
- Each and every interviewee, for your generosity of spirit and your willingness to share your life so that others might be helped and blessed by your life story.
- My wife Ruth, for your constant support and encouragement, and for typing the entire manuscript, including all the amendments.

1
'The best'

Glasgow is a splendid city. Its coat of arms bears the words 'Let Glasgow flourish'. It is a worthy motto, but it is only a part of the true message. Fourteen hundred years ago, a man called Kentigern led a Christian community and is now acknowledged as the founder of a village that eventually grew into the now great city.

Kentigern is better known by his pet name of Mungo. This godly man, now known as St Mungo, once said this about his place: 'Let Glasgow flourish, through the preaching of the Word and the praising of His Name.' That was his directive as he shared the good news of Jesus Christ, as well as his prayer for the people he loved and for whom he cared. The full quotation can be seen on the walls and interior glass of St George's Church in Tron, an area of Glasgow. However, the full words of Mungo are rarely used. Somehow, the 'God' bit gets lost.

In my own family, when I was a young man, something similar happened. My Christian parents were married for 25 years. When they reached this milestone, my father said to my mother:

Grow old along with me!
The best is yet to be.

1

These are the opening words of one of Robert Browning's most famous poems, 'Rabbi Ben Ezra'[1]. Of course it would have been tedious to quote the whole poem of 32 verses, but my father missed the best part, as the first verse in full says this:

> Grow old along with me!
> The best is yet to be,
> The last of life, for which the first was made:
> Our times are in His hand
> Who saith 'A whole I planned,
> Youth shows but half; trust God; see all, nor be
>   afraid!'

The tragedy was that my parents had less than one more year together before my mother died, very suddenly, aged 45. I am glad they did know their time was in God's hands, but my father missed that in his only quoting the first two lines.

This is a book about not leaving God out as we grow older. In our zeal for living, it is easy to sideline the One who wants to be there, with us and for us. As we grow older, we want to be faithful to our God, who is always faithful.

In the famous Yellowstone National Park in the state of Wyoming, USA, is a cone geyser which erupts dramatically but also predictably. The experts in the Park can forecast the next outburst, which saves visitors a great deal of standing around waiting. Its name is Old Faithful, and it is my prayer that all who read the chapters that follow, for whatever reason, may find that they can grow old and still remain faithful to their faithful God. If there be a reader who, as yet, does not have that relationship with the God who loves them, I pray that they will discover a true faith as they age.

There is much to think about, and, I confess, I am no great expert on every area that this book addresses. Dr Paul Tournier spent over 50 years as a general practitioner in Geneva before he wrote his wonderful book *Learning to Grow Old*[2], in which he said this:

> Retirement and old age, must, of course, be accepted. We have to give up all sorts of things, and accept with serenity the prospect of death, while remaining active, as sociable and friendly as we can, despite an unavoidable measure of loneliness. We must learn to use leisure profitably, take up new interests, interest ourselves in young people and new ideas. We must learn how to pray, how to meditate, how to acquire wisdom, how to be grateful. For its part, society must restore to the old their sense of their own value as human beings, and make them feel they are really accepted. It must also safeguard their dignity by means of adequate financial resources and personal attention.

These stirring words, written in 1971, are surely prophetic for our day. My aim is to explore all these aspects and several more. Others have written and spoken on this whole subject more ably than I can, and I have happily drawn on the expertise of many. There is much to consider, as I explore what 'old age' is and how ageing is often seen as a problem rather than an opportunity. We will find how God's view of older people is often diametrically opposed to society's approach. The attitude of the church is not always helpful, nor is our own. I will look at some of the older people in the Bible, many of whom did wonderful things, although a few messed things up. The question of what we can do in our later years is a challenge, which needs to be seen in the light of who we are to be, so our doing is motivated by the fire in our hearts.

A key factor to consider is whether or not we can change our lives and our life-style as we grow older. Is it possible to come to faith, to recover lost faith and to retain our faith in later life? I am happy to say that some very positive answers will emerge in all these areas. As an evangelist, I have to give some pointers as to how we can share our Christian faith as well. There is a need to look death in the face and see how we can die well; as Christians we have an eternal hope, so there will be a positive chapter about this.

Two areas which are especially challenging are those surrounding our health. The first is the one so much talked and written about – dementia. I have devoted a whole chapter to this, to see how we can cope. It leads into a further area of concern, that of caring for people whose lives deteriorate and who need care, with a look at how we can help those who do the caring.

As I have written, I also confess that I am personally involved in all I write; I am in my mid-70s, and the questions I pose need an answer for me, myself. As Lynda Gratton and Andrew Scott say about their recent book *The 100-Year Life*, so I have to say about this book:

This is a book about <u>you</u> and how you can plan your life. There will be more choices, and you will experience many changes. These are factors that bring into focus what you stand for, what you value and what you wish to base your life around.[3]

Theirs is very much a secular book, dealing primarily with money and work. By contrast, this is unashamedly Christian: hence the emphasis in the very next chapter.

Please come with me into the wonderful world of faith in our later years – so we can be sure of 'finishing well'.

2

'I'm glad I'm not young . . .'

Maurice Chevalier, who always gave the appearance of a happy, if somewhat elderly, French gentleman in his jauntily worn boater, once remarked, 'Old age isn't so bad when you consider the alternative.' On a first hearing this is slightly amusing, although, on second thought, it is a poor reflection both on being old and on dying. As if to contradict himself or, perhaps, confuse himself, Chevalier then sang 'I'm glad that I'm not young anymore' in his endearing performance in the film 'Gigi'[1]. He even confesses, in the song, that Methuselah is his patron saint!

Chevalier seems to have been confused by his experience. He reacts negatively to ageing in his personal comment, but more positively in his song. Getting older is confusing. It obviously raises the question 'What is old?' This is basic to everything in this book, but I do not want to answer it until I have looked at something even more fundamental: what is God's attitude to our ageing? His approach will colour our own view and, perhaps, help us to react as Chevalier did in his song, rather than in his more bleak personal comments.

It was the psalmist David who said of himself, 'I was young and now I am old' (Psalms 37.25). Was he happy about this? In the context of these words, it would seem he was. Speaking of the older person's problem of walking, literally as well as metaphorically, David has just said,

6

If the Lord delights in a man's way, he makes his steps
firm; though he stumble, he will not fall,
for the Lord upholds him with his hand. (37. 23–24).

Immediately after these words comes 'I was young, and now
I am old,' followed by

yet I have never seen the righteous forsaken
or their children begging for bread.
They are always generous and lend freely;
their children will be blessed.

For David, growing old was a good thing. Can it be the same
for us? Here are three big positives from God as we begin to
look at our own ageing.

God's saving presence

In my own growing old, I am hugely encouraged by God's
outstanding promise in Isaiah 46.4:

Even to your old age and grey hairs I am he, I am he
who will sustain you. I have made you and I will carry
you; I will sustain you and I will rescue you.

For a person who started to turn grey in his late thirties
and is now 'a whiter shade of pale' (as the 60s group Procol
Harum[2] sang), this has been good news for a long time. I
understand the need for some to keep a more youthful colour, but I rest content in the words of Proverbs 20.29:

The glory of young men is their strength,
grey hair is the splendour of the old.

I would like to feel the previous words of that book were true of me, but I have my doubts that Proverbs 16.31 is completely correct in my case:

Grey hair is a crown of splendour,
it is attained by a righteous life.

Whether I got my white hair from being good or not, I bask in the promises from God given in those verses from Isaiah. I am increasingly conscious of my personal need of God's 'rescue'. The famous, possibly apocryphal, story of the bishop on a train being accosted by an enthusiastic youngster with the question 'Are you saved?' which elicited the answer 'That all depends on what you mean by "saved"' would find an echo in me. The bishop continued, 'I have been saved, I am being saved and I will be saved.'

I was privileged to trust Christ with my life when only a boy, so in that sense, 'I have been saved'. Yet every day I feel the deep need for the 'rescue' Isaiah speaks of to enable me to be saved. I await the final dénouement of history, when 'I will be saved'. The promises of Psalm 91 are vital for my life, quoting from verses 1 and 2 and then verses 14 to 16:

He who dwells in the shelter of the Most High will rest in the shadow of the Almighty. I will say of the Lord, 'He is my refuge and fortress, my God in whom I trust.'

'Because he loves me', says the Lord, 'I will rescue him, for he acknowledges my name. He will call upon me and I will answer him; I will be with him in trouble, I will deliver him and honour him. With long life I will satisfy him and show him my salvation.'

I have never believed that to be 'saved' was only a one-off. I cannot, indeed must not, rely on an experience decades ago for my present relationship with God. We will see in Chapter 8 how it is still possible for those in later life to come into this 'salvation' for the first time, so do not despair if this includes you. But what a joy to know that the promise of salvation is for those who have 'a long life', and that this is a life which will 'satisfy'. This satisfaction takes us right into our eternal future, as Paul reminds us: 'Since we have now been justified by his [Christ's] blood, how much more shall we be saved from God's wrath through him! For if, when we were God's enemies, we were reconciled to him through the death of his Son, how much more, having been reconciled, shall we be saved through his life!' (Romans 5.9–10).

Reverting to the thought that this is an ongoing 'rescue' rather than a once-in-a-lifetime experience, our well-being depends on a continuing and continuous relationship with God, as he carries us and we trust him, as the writer of Proverbs enjoins us in Proverbs 3.1–4:

My son, do not forget my teaching, but keep my commands in your heart, for they will prolong your life many years and bring you prosperity. Let love and faithfulness never leave you; bind them round your neck, write them on the tablet of your heart. Then you will win favour and a good name in the sight of God and man.

This has always been the way we should live, as we enjoy God's presence. Right back during the exodus, Moses commands the people of Israel, in Deuteronomy 5.33:

Walk in all the way that the Lord your God has commanded you, so that you may live and prosper and prolong your days in the land that you will possess.

As we 'prolong' our own days, the advice from the recent book *The 100-Year Life* is for each of us: 'Regardless of whether you are 20, 40, or 60 you need to adjust to make the most of the gift of a longer life.'[3] As that is a wholly secular book, I would want to add the crucial caveat: we need to make sure we make the necessary adjustments with God's presence in our hearts.

One of the most brilliant works I have ever read is the book *Wind, Sand and Stars* by the French writer Antoine de Saint-Exupéry, at the end of which he tells of travelling on a train that is crammed full of hundreds of Polish workmen being sent home from France. He describes how he makes his way through the carriages, full of confused people, and finds a man and a woman with a child snuggled between them, fast asleep. He muses as to what this child could have become if he had been born in different circumstances, maybe growing to be a 'Mozart'. Alas, he explains, 'This little Mozart is condemned', as he 'will be shaped by the common stamping machine.' Having told his story, Saint-Exupéry concludes his whole remarkable book with these poignant words: 'Only the Spirit, if he breathe upon the clay, can create Man.'[4]

How much I need to let God's Holy Spirit continually

Breathe on me, breath of God
Fill me with life anew[5]

'Even to your old age and grey hairs . . . I will carry you . . . I will sustain you . . . I will rescue you.' Lord, make it true for me!

God's Purpose

I know a man who has recently retired from being a police officer. Despite having an interesting and varied job, he could not wait to get out. He counted down the months, then the days, then the hours until he finally left. He was free! I met him a few weeks later. 'I have nothing to do; I am so bored. I think I'll write a book.' I did not have the heart to tell him what that would mean. . . . Getting older is more than sitting around doing nothing, as he is discovering.

Dusty Springfield[6] complained that she didn't know what to do with herself – but I grew up in the Swingin' Sixties, when in my experience we all had plenty to do. We seemed to have boundless energy and there were never enough hours in the day – or the night. We were going to change the world, in the days when the times were a-changin', or so Bob

Dylan[7] told us. What happened? Maybe we did change a few things. We dared to do things with and for God, some of us, and many of our memories are good. Is that all we have now – memories? Are we to be like the retired policeman, bored and without purpose?

The answer is a resounding 'No!' The psalmist has some special and unique news for our later years (Psalms 92.12–15):

> The righteous will flourish like a palm tree, they will grow like a cedar of Lebanon; planted in the house of the Lord, they will flourish in the courts of our God. They will still bear fruit in old age, they will stay fresh and green, proclaiming 'The Lord is upright; he is my Rock, and there is no wickedness in him.'

There will be a complete chapter on the 'whats' of living our later years, but it is vital that, before we consider the 'can-dos', we realize this important point: God is not finished with us. In our later years, we are not only to be blessed but to be a blessing and bring a blessing. Life is no downward trend with God. He renews our life within us: 'So that your youth is renewed like the eagle's' (Psalms 103.5). This does not mean we have to be young all over again. That really would not be a good idea.

Tom Hanks' delightful film 'Big',[8] has Hanks playing Josh, who wishes to be big and to his amazement, suddenly becomes an 'adult'. His new life involves Susan, with whom he becomes romantically involved. The dénouement of the film is when (don't read this if you intend to watch the film!)

Josh realizes he wants to be back home with his mom and his old friend Billy. He invites Susan to come back with him and be a child again. Oh no, she says, she has been through all that once and could not face growing up again. Almost all of us would echo that. What then does it mean to have our youth renewed like an eagle's?

Consider the words of Psalm 92. In our youth we were 'fresh and green'. Sometimes that was in the wrong way, à la Cleopatra, speaking of

> My salad days
> When I was green in judgement, cold in blood,
> To say as I said then![9]

We did make mistakes. I go along with those who say, 'When I was young and foolish, I was young and foolish'. We were 'green' in a negative way. But that is not what the psalmist means. He is talking about how we grew and flourished, not just physically and mentally, but spiritually. We lived in the Springtime. Is it now Autumn, going into a desolate, leafless Winter? Is our spiritual life on a never-ending spiral of decline? If you believe that, come back again and again to these remarkable verses and see what God says.

The Psalm says we are to 'flourish like a palm tree'. I am frequently in very hot countries in equatorial Africa, where I see the different varieties of palms, enjoying the burning heat which attacks them, swaying in the tropical storms which batter them, yet producing delicious fruit. That is how the 'righteous' are to be in their later lives. They are to stand tall like the mighty cedars of Lebanon. In our lives we can do that, in our inmost beings, even when age bends our backs double. We can do this because we are 'planted in the house of the Lord' and we 'flourish in the courts of our God'. Stick in close with God the Father, through the presence in your life of Jesus Christ the Son and in the power of the Holy Spirit, and you will be fresh and green!

Some of the loveliest people I meet are well advanced in years, and yet they are clearly bearing 'fruit in old age'. The words of Paul in Galatians 5.22–23 are so well known and quoted regularly, but they are singularly appropriate to give a New Testament explanation of what it means to 'bear fruit in old age'. Paul speaks of the 'fruit of the Spirit' as comprising 'love, joy, peace, patience, kindness, goodness, faithfulness, gentleness and self-control' and says that 'Against such things there is no law.' The law of ageing is a law – and that law has no claim on our lives when God's Spirit is at work within us.

Louise Morse, in her book *What's Age Got to Do With It?*[10] writes on these verses, heading that section 'You are here on purpose, by divine design'[11]. We are to let God make us into beautiful older people. The world seems full of hatred; we show God's love. I have made it a practice to say 'I love you' to my children (all grown men) and my grandchildren. We do not have to go far to witness hatred; it is there on the television, when we go to a sports match, when we drive and get something slightly wrong and the fist is raised from the car driver we offended. My children face this continually – they need me to exhibit the fruit of love towards them. I should do so all the time by my actions and by my words frequently. My grandchildren often have a hard time at school; I should be the one with the hug of love.

Around is great sorrow and heartache; we are to demonstrate the Spirit's joy. I don't mean we should be forever grinning, although a gentle smile can lift a drooping heart. But we have God's help in our lives and have a way of coping in the sorrows everyone faces. David puts it like this: 'The Lord is my strength and my shield: my heart trusts in him, and I am helped. My heart leaps for joy and I will give thanks to him in song' (Psalm 28.7). Linked to this is the antidote to the war, violence and discord we see everywhere, as the Holy Spirit produces the fruit of peace in us. We can proclaim peace through the 'Prince of Peace' (Isaiah 9.6) and can be, ourselves, 'the peacemakers' (Matthew 5.9). Who will pour 'oil on troubled waters' if not us, with the oil of God's Spirit?

We will put up with life's problems with 'patience'. This is not one of my strengths, I confess! Too often I fail to see the stupidity of getting uptight and angry in a long queue at the check-out, or with a seemingly interminable traffic jam. But the fruit of the Spirit is 'patience'. I am glad that is it followed by 'kindness' and 'goodness'; in a seemingly uncaring and sinful world, these are such assets, traits of character which the Spirit alone can create in us.

With our partners and family and friends we exercise 'faithfulness', and in all our dealings there will be 'gentleness and self-control'. An impossible dream? No, says the psalmist, 'They will still bear fruit in old age' – the verb 'will' is a strong word.

The expression 'old wrinklies' is not particularly pleasant! By contrast, the 'oldies' of Psalm 92 'stay fresh and green'.

When the storms of life buffet, we can go well. Indeed, sometimes a good old battering can bring the best out of us. As Richard Ford says in his book *Let Me be Frank with You*:

> There's something to be said for a good no-nonsense hurricane, to bully life back into perspective.[11]

Perhaps you are bedridden as you read this—take comfort from Joel 2.28 and be one of those included there, where 'Your old men (and women) will dream dreams' and bless us as you tell of what you dreamt. There are those who would point out that Joel is referring specifically to prophetic dreams, which may not be for all of us. Whether this be so or not, we can all take heart from the words of Psalms 63.6: 'On my bed I remember you; I think of you through the watches of the night.' Here is our opportunity to do what the psalmist says we are to do, as we go about 'Proclaiming, "The Lord is upright; he is my Rock, and there is no wickedness in him."' (Psalms 92.15).

In the previous section about God's saving presence, I looked at some verses from Proverbs to speak of my white hair and how God's presence is with me now I am older. But those verses (Proverbs 16.31 and 20.29), as well as Psalm 92, say something just as important about God's purpose for us. As we get older, part of the fruit is that we give a powerful testimony:

> They will still bear fruit in old age, they will stay fresh and green, proclaiming, 'The Lord is upright; he is my Rock, and there is no wickedness in him' (Psalms 92.14-15).

That is the impact of these verses from Proverbs:

> Grey hair is a crown of splendour;
> it is attained by a righteous life (Proverbs 20.29).

> The glory of young men is their strength,
> grey hair is the splendour of the old!
>   (Proverbs 20.29).

Our older lives are to show that God gives us a wisdom from himself as we age. Job 12.12 asks,

> Is not wisdom found among the aged?
> Does not long life bring understanding?

God's purpose for us is to show, as we get older, that he gives us his strength and, through our experiences of him, his wisdom. 'Grey hair' should mean that we have this wisdom through the experience of life. One of the laws given to the people of Israel puts it strongly:

> Rise in the presence of the aged, show respect for the elderly and revere your God. I am the Lord (Leviticus 19:32).

In other words, we older people really do matter, hence the call for respect. We are there, both to bear fruit and also to use our wisdom to give counsel and leadership, perhaps not in the formal way of church leaders, but by our loving and caring advice and encouragement. We are to declare God's

17

power 'to the next generation': Psalms 71.18. Psalm 71 is written by an old man, as verse 18 shows. The psalmist says how he declares God's 'splendour all day long' (v.8), tells of God's righteousness and salvation (v.15), proclaims his 'mighty acts' (v.16), praises God (v.22) and speaks out God's good news (vs. 23–24). What a lot of things we can do: from praise to evangelism, from counsel to encouragement. 'We will tell the next generation (Psalms 78.4).'

There is a simple question, which Gratton and Scott present when introducing their book, that suggests that coming generations will live to be at least 100 years old. 'How will you make the most of this gift?'[12] They go on to say,

> A long life is a gift, not a curse. It is full of possibilities, and the gift is the gift of time. How you choose to use and structure that time is at the heart of the response to living longer.[13]

God has a purpose for each one of us, whatever our age. There is no moment in our lives when he draws a line and says, 'That's it. You have no purpose here anymore.' Except that, one day, he will call 'Time' for each of us—but that is for the next section, so let's get there.

God's peace

As Abraham grows old, God makes a beautiful promise to him. He shares with Abraham that future generations will have many troubles, but he gives this assurance to his 'friend', as he is described in James 2.23:

> You, however, will go to your fathers in peace and be buried at a good old age.

These lovely words, in Genesis 15.15, are for us too. I am looking at the impending deaths of each of us in Chapter 11, but, as I have already said, it is so important to get the principle stated right at the outset. Death has been beaten. Jesus has done it. Here are stirring words from Paul in 2 Corinthians 4.16–18:

> Therefore we do not lose heart. Though outwardly we are wasting away, yet inwardly we are being renewed day by day. For our light and monetary troubles are achieving for us an eternal glory that far outweighs them all. So we fix our eyes, not on what is seen, but on what is unseen. For what is seen is temporary, but what is unseen is eternal.

When Jesus rose from the dead, it was as if God, at the moment of the resurrection, looked into the tomb of his dead Son and called out, 'You have beaten sin! You have beaten death! You have beaten hell! Come back from the dead and live forever!' The disciples feared for the worst, so the very first word Jesus spoke to them was 'Peace' (Luke 24.36). He had already promised this to them before he died. In John 14.27 he told them,

> Peace I leave with you; my peace I give you. I do not give to you as the world gives. Do not let your hearts be troubled and do not be afraid.

We need to appropriate the words of Jesus for ourselves, taking on board the magnificent words of Paul. It will save us from the danger of always harking back to 'the good old days', as if our lives will never be so good now, causing us to lose our peace:

> Do not say, 'Why were the old days better than these?'
> For it is not wise to ask such questions (Ecclesiastes 7.10).

We can, with Paul, say, 'I have learned to be content whatever the circumstances' (Philippians 4.11). And this peace can transform us as we approach our own death.

I had a most gentle uncle, my father's younger brother, who was also my godfather. Uncle Douglas was one of life's encouragers. He had trusted Christ when a relatively young man, and he and my Aunt Daphne were the embodiment of the enjoinder to 'practice hospitality' (Romans 12.13). In his late eighties Douglas was found to have an aortic aneurism which, because of his age and its position, was inoperable. One Saturday afternoon I was called by my cousin Stephen from Doncaster.

> 'Dad's dying', he said. 'He wanted to see you before he
> goes – can you come, please?'
> 'How soon shall I be needed?'
> 'Oh, tomorrow's fine.'

I put the phone down and looked at my wise, Christian wife. 'Go now', was all she said. As I was on the 150-mile journey, unknown to me, Stephen called again, asking whether I could come any earlier. Ruth told him I would be already halfway there, and Stephen relayed this to his father. I arrived and was ushered straight into the hospital room. After brief greetings, I went over to my uncle's bed. I held his hand, asked him if he could hear me and received a reassuring squeeze.

'Douglas', I said, 'I know you are ready to die, but I would like to pray a blessing on you. Do you follow me?' Again, my hand was gripped. It was the greatest privilege to place my other hand gently on his head and then pray the great priestly blessing from Numbers 6.24–26:

> The Lord bless you and keep you;
> the Lord make his face shine upon you
> and be gracious to you;
> the Lord turn his face towards you
> and give you peace.

Douglas squeezed my hand one last time, and I bent and kissed him. I slipped quietly from the room, leaving his own immediate family with him. He died within ten minutes. He had waited for the blessing of peace and was able to die in the complete certainty that all was well. I do miss this dear man, but I saw what God promised to Abraham to be true for my Uncle Douglas, and he had his funeral in 'a good old age'.

He, like others who have died trusting in Jesus Christ, proved for himself the truth of Paul's words, which follow directly after the ones quoted above:

Now we know that if the earthly tent we live in is destroyed, we have a building from God, an eternal house in heaven, not built by human hands. (2 Corinthians 5.1)

I will expand on this later, but it is vital for our wellbeing that we ask God for this to be an assurance deep in our hearts. My mother was a Williams from Holyhead, an island adjoining Anglesey in North Wales. I am therefore somewhat biased towards the hymns of William Williams, the most famous of which is 'Guide Me, O Thou Great Jehovah', written in Welsh in 1745 and translated into English by Peter Williams. In most versions, the third and final verse says this:

When I tread the verge of Jordan,
Bid my anxious fears subside;
Death of deaths, and hell's destruction,
Land me safe on Canaan's side,
Songs of praises, songs of praises,
I will ever give to Thee,
I will ever give to Thee.[14]

Magnificent hymns, with last lines repeated again and again, are one thing; their experience in our lives is another. The first Earl Cairns (1819 to 1885) was an Irish statesman, a leading lawyer and Lord Chancellor in 1868 and from 1874 to 1880. With all his fame, one thing marked his life more than anything else. When he was a small boy, someone said to him, 'God claims you'. He asked his mother about this, and she, in return, asked him, 'What are you going to do about the claim?' His response was to change his life: 'I shall own it, and give myself to him.'

In the same way, we must claim God's promises for ourselves. As Charles Wesley wrote in his hymn 'And Can It Be':

> No condemnation now I dread;
> Jesus and all in Him, is mine!
> Alive in Him, my living Head,
> And clothed in righteousness Divine.
> Bold I approach the eternal throne,
> And claim the crown, through Christ my own.[15]

If we are to live well and then die well, like Wesley celebrating his conversion in 1738 with that hymn or like Earl Cairns, we need to 'own the claim'. We must say for ourselves, with the psalmist, 'Even when I am old and grey, do not forsake me, O God.' (Psalms 71.18).

As a final word of encouragement to conclude this chapter, consider this:

God is not old

Michelangelo and Leonardo da Vinci have a lot to answer for. Their depictions of God, in the case of Michelangelo, and Jesus, by da Vinci, are the most replicated religious pictures of all time and have had a profound influence on the way we visualize God the Father and God the Son.

The phenomenal fresco 'The Last Supper' by Leonardo da Vinci covers a complete wall at one end of the refectory in the Convent of Santa Maria delle Grazie in Milan. It really is a 'must see', deeply moving and inspiring, measuring 15 by 29 feet and painstakingly restored. Even in a somewhat crumbling condition when I saw it some years ago, it was magnificent. However, it is one man's interpretation of the Last Supper. Countless artists have imitated this style in which Jesus is pictured, which may or may not be a good thing, because he may or may not have looked anything like da Vinci saw him.

I have also gazed at the ceiling of the Sistine Chapel in the Apostolic Palace in Vatican City. The entire ceiling is one huge and continuous painting by Michelangelo. Necks are craned, voices raised (only to be shushed by overzealous attendants) and illicit photos secretly taken of a range of biblical scenes, dominated by the story of creation from the book of Genesis. Although it is only the fourth of the creation panels, the one which stands out above all others is the creation of Man, where God touches with his outstretched fingers the similarly outstretched fingers of Adam, giving him life – which creates, not just life, but an enormous problem.

Why has Michelangelo painted the two figures as he has? Was Man as young, muscular and fair as that? More vital than that, is God an old man with white hair, a white beard and a flowing white tunic? It is not just the contrast which is so apparent; it is the 'oldness' of God that has been copied ever since, as if God is an old man. Right down to today, this image continues. When a famous entertainer died on 18 August 2017, several newspapers, not least *The Times*[16], carried cartoons depicting God, complete with flowing white hair and beard and sitting on a fluffy white cloud, greeting the entertainer with the latter's catchphrase, 'Nice to see you, to see you nice': the farewell to Sir Bruce Forsyth.

Leonardo da Vinci and Michelangelo: wonderful artists, but causes of misconceptions as to what the Deity is really like. For 'No one has ever seen God' (John 1.18), and even though that verse continues 'God the One and Only, who is at the Father's side, has made him known,' no one knows what Jesus looks like either. I do like the story of the little girl at school; in class painting a picture, she was asked by the teacher what she was producing. 'It's going to be God,' the girl said. 'But no one knows what God looks like,' came the reply, which evoked the delightful response, 'I haven't finished my picture yet!'

All this leads me to the salient point: the Bible makes it clear that God is not an old person getting older. It is true he is described as having white hair in the dramatic vision of Daniel (Daniel 7.9):

The Ancient of Days took his seat. His clothing was as white as snow, the hair of his head was white like wool. His throne was flaming with fire and its wheels were all ablaze.

The similarity with John's vision of Jesus in the first chapter of Revelation is obvious, where Jesus is described as having 'a robe reaching down to his feet . . . his head and hair were white like wool, as white as snow, and his eyes were like a blazing fire' (Revelation 1.13–14). The point of both visions is the purity and power of God, not his longevity.

However, calling God 'the Ancient of Days' must say something significant in the words used. God must clearly have designed ageing, and he honours the aged. Time does pass, from the very creation of day and night (Genesis 1.5) and, therefore, everything ages. God is not old as we understand 'old', but he is venerable, and his title here validates age as something of great worth and significance. We should reflect this, both in society and in the church.

Having said that, God is not ageing as we and our world get older. 'I the Lord do not change' is his own statement in Malachi 3.6. 'Jesus Christ is the same yesterday and today and forever,' Hebrews 13.8 proclaims. This means that the God of Creation had not been old then and is getting older, but is the same as he has always been. That leads to the stupendous news that he is always there, always reliable, not fading slowly away as we are. When he promises

Never will I leave you,
never will I forsake you

in Hebrews 13.5, it makes him different from everyone we know and different from us ourselves. One of these days, our nearest and dearest will die – or we will. They, or we, will not always be around. But God will. He will always be our helper. Commenting on this verse, Louise Morse and Roger Hitchings say this:

Christ . . . has promised that he will never leave us. Our older folk have a good deal of life experience, and have gone through the 'deep waters' and one of the joys of talking with them is hearing how God has made Himself felt in all their circumstances, large and small.[17]

This everlastingness of God, his changelessness, means that we who age can know there is one on whom we can rely totally who is outside the restraints of space and time. Others may let us down or leave us. As for God, Lamentations 3.22–23 gives us this assurance about him:

His compassions never fail. They are new every morning; great is your faithfulness.

The hymn writer Henry Francis Lyle lay dying from tuberculosis in 1847. He read the request of two disciples to Jesus on the road to Emmaus, 'Stay with us, for it is nearly evening' (Luke 24.29) and penned his hymn, 'Abide With Me, Fast Falls the Eventide',[18] the second verse saying this:

Swift to its close ebbs out life's little day;
Earth's joys grow dim; its glories pass away;
Change and decay in all around I see;
O Thou who changest not, abide with me.

Lyle went on in his hymn to say what a difference this made, as he feared no foe, no bitterness of tears, and that death had lost its sting (a reference to 1 Corinthians 15.55). Growing older and facing death itself can be good experiences, because we have a changeless God who loves us and cares for us. Perhaps we will even dare to enjoy the fact that we may actually be 'old', as the next chapter will explore.

3

Will you still need me?

We were sitting together in her living room. My Gran held my hand, and her face took on a look of sadness tinged with pity. She began to shake her head. 'Ian', she said, 'There are some old people in our church,' emphasizing the word 'old'. It was clear that not only did she feel they had no hope, but also that she did not in any way associate herself with their company. I was at a loss as to how to reply, as my Gran was 95 at the time. Old? Not her. She lived for another six years, and I only saw her being 'old' in the last six months.[1]

In researching for this book, I have found I have to be careful what I say when telling almost anyone over about 40 that I am questioning 'when' and 'who' is old. The older someone is, the more they will bristle with indignation at the very idea that they might be included in the term. A typical short exchange invariably goes like this:

Them: 'What's new in your life?'
Me: 'I'm writing a book.'
Them: 'Oh – what about?'
Me: 'About faith in later years.'
Them: 'Goodness! What's later years?'
Me: 'When you get older.'
Them: 'Well, count me out – I'm not old!'

If my Gran did not consider herself old at 95 – and very few of the many people I have interviewed accept that they are old – then, when is 'old'?

When is 'old'?

The question 'When is "old"?' does not have a straightforward answer. It partly depends on who is answering. I well recall the time I first became a youth leader, as opposed to a Sunday School teacher. I was 20, and to tell the whole truth, I was really an assistant youth leader. George Green was the main leader, a man of great age and experience and, in my view at the time, something of a miracle himself at being able to communicate with teenagers at his time of life. He was – unbelievably – twice my age. As you would expect, when I reached the advanced age of 40, I understood perfectly how young George had been and how silly had been my judgement. Now I am in my seventies; no wonder my grandchildren consider me ancient.

Is it possible old age begins as young as 40? Shakespeare, in one of his sonnets, seemed to think so:

When forty winters shall besiege thy brow
And dig deep trenches in thy beauty's field[2]

Daisy Ashford, in her first novel, has as one of her characters a Mr Salteena, described as 'an elderly gentleman of forty-two'.[3] It should be pointed out that Daisy did write that novel at the age of 12 and published it in 1919! Accepting that the young view those older as 'past it', they and we need to heed the words of Atul Gawande in his book *Being Mortal*: 'There's no escaping from the tragedy of life, which is that we are all aging from the day we are born.'[4] Gawande is giving, in what is a good and thoughtful book, a non-Christian analysis. As we will see, ageing does not have to be a tragedy. From the beginning of creation, everything has aged. Ageing in itself is not the problem; the problem is ageing in a fallen world.

Henri Nouwen, in his sometimes moving book *Our Greatest Gift*, narrates a time when he was chatting with a university student who told Nouwen that his father did not understand him. His father always had to be right, never allowing the student any room for his own ideas. Nouwen counselled that his own father was not very different, telling the student, 'That's the older generation.' The student gave a sigh and replied, 'Yes, my dad is already 40!' Nouwen concludes this little story with a wry observation: 'I suddenly realized that I was speaking to someone who could have been my grandson.'[5]

> That youth at us should have its fling
> Is hard on us, is hard on us
> To our prerogative we cling
> So pardon us, so pardon us
> If we decline to dance and sing

lamented Pooh-Bah, the grandee of Gilbert and Sullivan's *Mikado*.[6]

It would be easy to blame the 'youth' for calling us old. But where shall we start in any attempt to define the word?

To begin with, I turn to a most learned tome, which bears the grandiose title *Psychodynamic Diagnostic Manual: Second Edition*, known by the abbreviation PDM2 (which I will use hereafter), published in 2017.[7] In one of its many sections, it deals with what it calls 'older adults'. Under the sub-heading 'Classification of older adults', the writers say,

> While there is no biological or psychological parameter that defines 'old', it has been generally accepted that old age begins at 65 years. For clinical purposes, an accepted cut-off has been even younger, 55 years of age. Indeed, a recent epidemiological study of mental disorders in older adults in the United States . . . divided the elderly into four groups: 'young-old' (55-64 years of age), 'middle-old' (65-74 years of age), 'old-old' (75-84 years of age), and 'oldest-old' (85 years of age and older).

Not so very long ago, the then government in the United Kingdom had a policy initiative entitled 'Life Begins at 50: A Better Society for Older People', which then Prime Minister Tony Blair commended, saying he was 'pleased that the saying "life begins at 50" has been chosen as the title of this report.'[8]

Should we, therefore, choose an age as a starting point? Most would think that the government's suggestion of 50 was very young. By contrast, Louise Morse cites a newspaper article (unspecified), with a heading 'Why old age starts at 85',[9] which might be considered way too high. Is it a question of a certain age, or is it more complex?

In my previous book *Older People and the Church*,[10] I quoted a lengthy but excellent piece of writing by Robert

Katz, who looked at the socio psychological perspectives of ageing:

Despite vast medical progress we know relatively little about the phenomenon of aging. The term itself is imprecise and ambiguous. We do know some things about the processes of aging, one of these being that we begin to 'age' while we are still in our late teens. We age at different rates; aging has different meanings for different people; to be aged may be a chronological variable because Picasso at ninety-plus had more vigour than some of us who would be loosely categorised as being of 'middle-age'. Medical researchers only recently discovered that the arteries of young men can be 'aged', while some people attain a 'ripe old age' with cardiovascular systems resembling those associated with much younger people. Are we aged if we choose to retire at the age of forty-five or fifty, or are we 'aged' when we first become eligible for social security? Do we become 'aged' when we leave our own apartment and move into a residence complex where our fellow residents are classified as being 'elderly'? There simply is no unequivocal meaning for the 'aging' or 'aged'; moreover, we cannot be sure when we are speaking in the language of physiology, psychology, economic status, athletic ability and physical co-ordination, medicine and health status, political influence, familial role, or something else. More than most of us realize, aging is a state of mind; we are what *we* think we are, the ways we perceive ourselves, and the ways we imagine our family and our community to perceive us. Aging is, at the very least a relative term.[11]

A quotation of this length speaks for itself and gives the helpful view that, as we often say, 'it all depends.' Most readers will have recognized the words which headed this chapter and, if an age has to be used for the start of old age, especially when even the pensionable age is being moved time and time again to save money, maybe the Beatles got it right, as the following shows.[12] On a requests programme on Classic FM, in November 2017, a lady's choice of music (classical, not the Beatles!) was dedicated to her husband on his birthday, with the words, 'Yes, I still need you, yes, I'll still feed you, now you're 64!'

With good grace or a grumpy frown, perhaps we will have to admit that '64' is a reasonable starting point. Before we leave this thorny question, let me put it another way:

Who is old?

The disciples of Jesus asked him, in a completely different context and about something totally different, 'Surely not I?' (Matthew 26.22). Even guilty Judas Iscariot asked that (verse 25). Surely, in our current context, surely not I? Perhaps I need to echo the words of Henri Nouwen:

It helps me to look at myself in the mirror once in a while. Gazing at my face, I see both my mother and my father when they were sixty years old, and I remember how I thought of them as old people.[13]

My own mother died without a white strand in her raven Welsh hair, aged 45, so I cannot do that with her. But my father, alas, has given me a face just like his. I may get out of bed feeling young – but the mirror is my father looking back at me, and I am the older person I pretend not to be.

In the same way as we cloak death with euphemisms to make it more acceptable ('passed on', 'gone to Glory' and so on), we fudge the word 'old' with slightly more pleasant alternatives. In her book 'Three Score Years – and Then?' the late Rhena Taylor gives us plenty of choices as she talks about evangelism:

> No one likes admitting to being 'old' these days, so what can we call our 'target audience'? Is 'older people' all right? If not; the elderly? Over 60's? Those in later life/years? Mature citizens? Retired people? The aged? Seniors? Senior citizens? Pensioners? Chronologically disadvantaged/advantaged? There seems no end to the efforts we make to get it right and I am only listing, as I'm sure you realize, the politer terms used.[14]

Taylor agrees that the problem is aggravated 'Because we are talking of a possible age range of forty years, and several generations' and suggests we use the term 'the third age' and 'the fourth age', defining people 'not by age, but by health and fitness'.[15] Health is certainly a factor which may determine whether I am old or not. We all know people who are prematurely old through ill health and others who seem to have boundless energy and a youthful attitude that belies their chronological age. Louise Morse puts it well: 'What really matters isn't so much the state of the body, but the health of the soul and the spirit!'[16]

However we understand what is 'old' and who comes within that term, the worst thing would be to overgeneralize. Rob Merchant has a helpful comment:

> One of the difficulties when we start thinking of older people is that this segment of the population suddenly starts to become one large amorphous blob, lacking distinction or boundaries.[17]

He has a rather good turn of phrase. Old? What I think may not be what others say. Perhaps we need to hear the reply given by Arthur, in the film of the same title, to his butler, Hobson, in the following exchange:

> Arthur: 'Do you want anything?'
> Hobson: 'I want to be younger.'
> Arthur: 'Sorry, it's your job to be older.'[18]

Perhaps that's it. It's an inevitable part of life to grow old! But now comes the really scary part: there are a very great many of us, and our numbers are growing alarmingly.

The statistics

I want to enter a word of caution before unleashing the facts. What follows is not all our fault. The young are at least partly to blame. They are not making enough babies, and as a result of which, there is an imbalance of older people in the population and our numbers are seen as disproportionately high. The medical doctor Paul Tournier, admittedly writing in the 1970s, makes that point:

> I used to think, naïvely, that this great number of old people was a flattering proof of the progress of medicine, which today saves so many patients who only a few years ago would inevitably have died. Not at all! According to Alfred Sauvy, it is the falling birth rate which up to now has been the specific cause of the aging of populations. Paul Paillat is even more categorical. He quotes the work of Bourgeous-Pichat, who was, as he says, 'the first to demonstrate that the sole cause of the aging in our society is the fall in the birth rate' . . . So much for my vanity as a doctor![19]

There are vast numbers of statistics to show that a veritable army of us are old, which should encourage us to see, as we go on to look at our potential, what we might achieve together. Instead of drip-feeding these around the book, here are some figures which, when put together, I find quite scary. The very quantity of older people is remarkable: there are 11.8 million in the United Kingdom who are aged 65 and over.[20] When you take this back only five years to the over-sixties, the figure goes up to 15.3 million.[21] To go in the other direction, by the age of 85, there are still 1.6 million people,[22] which leads to those aged 90-plus numbering over half a million. In this last category, women form 70 per cent of the total.[23]

We are talking huge numbers here, and these numbers are increasing all the time – and rapidly. This is seen, perhaps most startlingly, in those who become centenarians, where the growth has been no less than 65 per cent in the last decade, to 14,570.[24] Of course, there does come a final slowing down, but there are still 800 who are aged 105 and over, a figure which has doubled since 2005.[25] Whichever way you look at it, the older generations are gaining ground.

Pausing here for a quirky fact: the Queen used to send telegrams to each person who reached one hundred years of age, and then each birthday after that. In the first year of her reign, she sent 134 such telegrams. As telegrams no longer exist, Her Majesty now sends a rather lovely card to each centenarian and another on each subsequent birthday. She now has to employ eight full-time card senders, there are so many recipients.

And there's more (to coin a phrase). Future predictions only emphasize the point just made: older age is a growth industry. The figure of 15.3 million aged 60-plus, quoted above, is projected to pass 20 million as early as 2030,[26] while those 65-plus will rise by the same date by over 40 per cent.[27] No wonder alarm bells are ringing in the government, the Health Services and elsewhere, because it is predicted that, by 2040, which is not very far away, almost one in four of the population (24.2 per cent), will be 65-plus.[28] It could be argued that we will be fitter, more able to work and capable of meaningful contributions to society in many ways, including financially, but there will, inevitably, be a time when we are much less able to do this. The prediction is that those who are 85 and over will double, by 2030, to 3.4 million,[29] while those of us who get to 75 and live on after that will double in the next 30 years.[30] This is serious growth, to put it mildly.

Pause again to consider this: by 2035, even with such predictions, the United Kingdom will actually be one of the least aged countries among the 27 countries currently in the European Union.[31] But there are some statistics that are possibly rather sad even in this more youthful country. Of all those over 65 years of age, 32 per cent will live alone.[32] Two million people over 75 live alone, of whom 1.5 million will be women.[33] The biggest prediction of all is this: nearly one in five of all those now living in the United Kingdom will reach 100, including 29 per cent of those born in 2011.

This book is not for the few: it is for all to read and take seriously. It is vital for society to get its act together. It is all the more important for the Church to do so. Alas, the views of both are not all they should be, as we shall now see.

4

'Darling, I am growing old'

Growing old is not a problem. When a friend of mine sees his little girl killed by his own car rolling down his drive and crushing her: that is a problem. When my mother dies of a heart attack at 45, leaving my father with four children, the youngest aged ten: that is a problem. When my brother Keith goes out to Uganda under the regime of Idi Amin to be a doctor there and dies at the age of 28: that is a problem. Young lives with so much potential, so many might-have-beens, so much grief at so-called 'untimely' deaths: these are problems that take a lot of years to resolve, if they are ever resolved.

On my visits to African countries, I have discovered that African Christians rarely, if ever, use the word 'problem'. Instead, they choose the word 'challenge'. School fees for the vast majority who are poor are cripplingly expensive and are compulsory in many countries at secondary school level. But they are not a problem; they are a challenge. Picking oneself up after a terrible bereavement, of which there are many, is a challenge. Ill health, which is common, is a challenge.

I am spelling all this out to make a serious point: growing old is not a problem. It may be seen as such, as I will now explore. However, it is a privilege to get older. I wish, more than I can say, that my mother and my brother had lived on for many years. They did not – but I have. I have a life to live and a God to love and serve. That is an honour. It is also a challenge. When my brother died, I felt he fell holding a torch that he carried for Jesus. I found myself being asked by God if I would take up that torch and run with it. I accepted that request and have now visited many countries in Africa over 50 times, including Uganda, where Keith worked, and Kenya, where he is buried. By God's grace, I continue this work into my seventies. It is not a problem; it is a privilege and a challenge.

There is a clear distinction between ageing being a problem or a challenge, shown by the following two quotations. The first is from Shakespeare's 'Macbeth', words spoken by Macbeth himself, after the death of his wife. The second is from a sermon preached by St Augustine. The difference between the two could hardly be more stark.

Tomorrow, and tomorrow and tomorrow,
Creeps in this petty pace from day to day.
To the last syllable of recorded time,
And all our yesterdays have lighted fools
The way to dusty death. Out, out brief candle!
Life's but a walking shadow, a poor player
That struts and frets his hour upon the stage
And then is heard no more: it is a tale
Told by an idiot, full of sound and fury,
Signifying nothing.[1]

Such negativity is understandable after a sudden, shocking bereavement, but it shows one way to face our latter days. Now here is Augustine:

> New indeed we ought to be, because the old man ought not to creep upon us, but we must grow and advance. Of this very advancement the Apostle (Paul) says, 'Though our outward man perish, yet our inward man is renewed every day.' Let us not grow old to become old after being new, but let newness itself grow.[2]

How do we grow old? Do we do it the Shakespeare way or the Augustine way? This needs to be answered by considering what are the opportunities. Because the opportunities are so great, as we will explore in Chapters 6 and 7, we can dare to look the challenge right in the face. It would be folly to ignore these challenges, as if all in the garden were rosy. Clive Dunn (of 'Dad's Army' fame) was told by the children who sang on his best-selling single 'Grandad' that he was someone they loved.[3]

But it is not always lovely or true. We can see this from three viewpoints: the way society views our ageing, the approach of the Church and then how we ourselves see it.

How society views ageing

The popularly held view of old age today is of very old people, usually women, living alone, socially isolated, managing on inadequate incomes, poorly housed, suffering ill-health, dependent on young carers, yet isolated from their families. Unhappy, withdrawn, but at the same time not taking an interest in making new friends, they have lost their energy, enthusiasm and drive, and are no longer concerned with education or personal development. Their deteriorating physical and mental health offers only the prospect of further decline and the ultimate sentence of old age – death.[4]

These sobering words, in a publication by Age Concern in 1990, itself with a serious title, 'Age: The Unrecognised Discrimination' set out clearly our first challenge: society views ageing in a negative way. 'Ageism' is a comparatively new word, first defined by Robert Butler in 1969 as a stereo-typing of and discriminating against individuals or groups on the basis of their age.[5] He explained this further in the *Encyclopaedia of Aging* in 1987, using his original words with this explanation:

Ageism is defined as a process of systematic stereotyping of, and discrimination against, people because they are old, just as racism or sexism accomplish this for skin colour and gender.'[6]

It will be seen at once how dangerous this is for all who behave in this way; whoever is 'ageist' will, given time, fall victim to their own prejudices. I will not change my skin colour, nor (except in rare circumstances) my sex, but I will age.[7] Almost every book or article written about growing old stresses this as a major problem. Morse and Hitchings say that

Ageism is endemic in the U.K., with older people being judged as having no value as they are not seen as contributors to society. Their charitable work, and their support for their families and churches is usually overlooked.[8]

Writing on her own, Louise Morse asserts 'ageism and age discrimination [are] like pollution, lurking unseen, every-where.'[9] Tom Kitwood, writing over 20 years ago, agrees:

Many societies, including our own, are permeated by an ageism which categorises older people as incompetent, ugly and burdensome, and which discriminates against them at both a personal and structural level.[10]

All these writers I have quoted are learned people who have researched this subject with great care and have not written lightly, nor from anger. There seems to be a view of ageing that is frequently negative. The great Irish poet W.B. Yeats, in his masterly 'Sailing to Byzantium', starts his second verse with these words:

An aged man is but a paltry thing,
A tattered coat upon a stick.[11]

In the most subtle of ways, old age is perceived to bring its problems and be seen negatively. Take, as an example, that most famous of verses, used every Remembrance Day in November, published first in *The Times* at the beginning of the First World War in 1914. The whole poem, by Robert

Laurence Binyon (1869-1943) is entitled 'For the Fallen', with verse four being the one we all know:

> They shall grow not old, as we that are left grow old:
> Age shall not weary them, nor the years condemn.
> At the going down of the sun and in the morning
> We will remember them.[12]

These moving words are always seen as a tribute to those who have given their lives, usually at a young age, in war. However, the prospect for those who are left is discouraging, even bleak. 'Age' is going to 'weary them', while 'the years condemn'. Is that how Binyon sees his own ageing? Apparently it is. Somehow, society's attitude takes up this theme, seeing an impending crisis in an increasingly ageing population, where older people are a burden.[13] Given the sense of crisis, we might expect considerable resources to be devoted to the study of old age. Instead, there is a lack of research, a lack which itself may be a result of ageism. Those doing research even at the highest level regret the lack of others' research, as PDM-2 states:

> Unfortunately, there is a paucity of empirical research on older adults in general, and specifically on psychodynamic aspects of aging . . . This is due, in part at least, to an unfortunate cycle in which older adults have often been excluded from clinical research studies.[14]

This should not be so. It is part of a hidden discrimination, which is highlighted in recent statistics. Within the last ten years, figures that are of a great concern have been published.

These show that, in England, of all those aged 65 and over, no less that 36.8 per cent say they have experienced some form of discrimination.[15] When this age is taken upwards to those aged 70 to 79, the figure increases to 37.2 per cent.[16] Sadly, as high a percentage as 76 per cent of older people believe that the country fails to make good use of their talents,[17] while 53 per cent of all adults believe that, if they reach old age, they will be treated like children,[18] which is a cause for pessimism.

Because of all this, everything is coloured with the dye of ageing. When I go to a well-known chemist to get some cream for my wife's face, the shop assistant takes one look at me and concludes, 'You'll be looking for anti-ageing cream.' When I assure her that my wife is some years younger than I and is happy to be getting older, so I only want skin cream, the young lady looks at me as if I am crazy. 'No', she says, 'we only have anti-ageing cream.' 'But . . .' I begin to reply – and give up. The assumption is that creams are not to smooth our skins; they are to stop us getting older. 'It is this "dread of ageing" that underpins ageism, affecting attitudes towards older age and therefore towards older people themselves,' says Rob Merchant.[19] As Nouwen and Gaffney comment,

We might think that becoming old is the same as becoming a problem, that aging is a sad human fate that nobody can escape and should be avoided at all cost, that growing towards the end of the life cycle is a morbid reality that should only be acknowledged when the signs can no longer be denied. Then all our concerns for the elderly become like almsgiving with a guilty conscience, like friendly gestures to the prisoners of our war against aging.[20]

Simone de Beauvoir puts it even more strongly in her pessimistic book *The Coming of Age*:

> The vast majority of mankind looks upon the coming of old age with sorrow and rebellion. It fills them with more aversion than death itself.[21]

These are the last words of her long book: what a conclusion! Thus, old age is seen as decline and loss, not for its gains and achievements.[22] Whatever we older people give, it is what we take that is noticed by society, as Laslett pointed out 30 years ago:

> In our own country at the moment all that we seem able to see is the ever growing number of failing elderly people who weigh upon the individuals who support them. Ageing is seen as a burden on society at large because resources have to be found to give older people incomes, provide for their ever-failing health, to maintain institutions for those who cannot be supported otherwise.[23]

Notice Laslett's reference to 'our country', because it may be singularly significant. The approach in the UK (and apparently, across other Western countries) is in stark contrast with what I and others see elsewhere. As I travel extensively in several countries in Africa, it is my experience that those who are older are, by and large, highly regarded. My white hair is an 'open sesame' for respect and a desire to hear from a person with an experience of life, coupled with knowledge. I fear I am nowhere as good as they believe, but my age is a bonus. I see this respect for all who are in their later days, regardless of their abilities.

It was the same when I visited various parts of India: an acknowledgement that old age was to be valued and appreciated. In his powerful book *Being Mortal*, written from an American perspective, Atul Gawande writes of the shock his Indian father found after he had moved from his country of birth to the United States. This ageing father was thrilled to be made an American citizen, and he loved so much of his new nationality. Then Gawande says this:

> But one thing he could never get used to was how we treat our old and frail – leaving them to a life alone or isolating them in a series of anonymous facilities, their last conscious moments spent with nurses and doctors who barely knew their names. Nothing could have been more different from the world he grew up in.[24]

As part of the extensive research done for PDM-2, the authors, using their own sources, which I am omitting, also find major differences between East and West:

> In Western cultures, there is an emphasis on youth, beauty, independence and productivity. In Eastern

47

cultures, there is more of a sense of duty, harmony and respect for elders, and dependence is less stigmatized. In Eastern cultures, loss of cognitive skills is not considered as pathological as in Western societies, so there is greater tolerance for cognitively impaired elders.[25]

My question would be this: will this positive attitude continue in these African and Asian situations into the future? I think it possible that, with rapid globalization and, throughout these areas, a huge move from the countryside into vast cities, the Western approach will become universal. In the extensive and forward-looking book *The 100-Year Life*, the authors have a section entitled 'Multi-generational living'. As their experience is very akin to mine in Africa, the following is pertinent:

When we visit Asia, particularly India, we are struck by something we rarely see in the West: children, parents and grandparents living together. When we talk to friends in multi-generational families, they talk positively of the many advantages. Children have an opportunity to spend time with their grandparents, the parents feel they have more support when they are working, and elderly relations feel they have a positive role and contribution to make. Indeed, there is a growing body of research that shows that multi-generational relationships can boost longevity. Loneliness in old age is a killer, and there are real advantages for the elderly to be embedded in their families. Of course, our Asian hosts also mention the downside: a lack of privacy and the possibility of caustic relations between the generations.[26]

How different from the way we live in the West! I wonder if the multicultural society that now exists in great swathes of the UK will enable the good from the East and Africa to influence our society for the better – or will the opposite happen? At present, as Tournier observes, 'Our Western outlook is quite the opposite.'[27] Time will tell if the West benefits from what the East has to teach us. But I am not holding my breath.

Perhaps we who are old can show, by our lifestyle and positive attitude, that things can change. Our good example could make a difference. In an article in *The Times* on the first day of 2018, Shane Watson made some tongue-in-cheek predictions for the New Year.[28] One he calls 'zero tolerance of ageism', following the impact of David Attenborough's latest nature series and the success of 59-year-old Debbie McGee on 'Strictly Come Dancing'. He admits that 'this could be wishful midlife thinking', but change may be coming. We will pursue this is the next chapter. But, first, a look at the second of our three areas.

How the Church views ageing

Before we face some of the challenges found in the relationship between the Church and those of us in our later years, we need to have an idea as to what we mean when we use the very word 'church'. In my previous book *Older People and the Church*,[29] my research then uncovered over 60 definitions of the term from those I interviewed. So to claim that 'the Church' has a particular approach to older people is to go down a tricky road, for it all depends on who is defining the word. Is it an 'insider' or one who, like Oscar Wilde (later adopted by Winston Churchill as his position), says, 'I'm not a pillar of the Church but more a flying buttress – I support it from the outside'?

What follows in the next few paragraphs may seem somewhat tortuous. As I will explain, what the New Testament teaches about the meaning of 'church' is not the way many see it now. I say now, as I will reiterate, that the biblical meaning of 'church' is the gathered people of God. But we do need to see what others think, if we are to help them. For example, in the village where I live, there is only one 'church' – the one near the end of our main street. There are folk in the village who depart for nearby towns, villages and even 40 miles away to our county's only city on a Sunday to worship: Baptists, Roman Catholics, Pentecostals and so on, but the villagers look to the solitary building that is, almost inevitably, Church of England, with its tower dating back a thousand years. It is here we 'hatch 'em, match 'em and despatch 'em' with our christenings, marriages and funerals. For most people who ever give it a thought, which on the surface seems to be fewer and fewer, the building is 'church'.

At the other end of the spectrum, many would prefer to think of 'church' as the gathered people of God. The hopes of those who have asked for this book to be written include the need for a theology of community and intergenerational relationships within that community, so that there is a theology of 'church' that sets out these intergenerational relationships as God intended. This, I was instructed, was to include a theology of usefulness in church that explains the positive role of older people even as mental and physical capabilities decline.

People have different definitions of church, which include the building itself, a gathering like a home and a family, a place of safety and an open door of welcome. Church for some is worship; for others it is the fellowship.[30] Whether church is seen as the building or, as the New Testament sees it, as the gathering of the people of God, we do need to bear in mind this multi-faceted and multi-coloured diversity when we discuss 'the Church'. However, it is crucial that we try to adhere to the Bible's definition of the Church as people seeking to be God's people.

For our current purposes, accepting that all 'churches' have to meet somewhere, so the 'building' aspect applies even if the church is in someone's home, I am taking the view that, more than anything, 'church' is the people who are seeking to be God's people. Now comes the big question: how does the Church feel about those of us who are getting older? Conversely, how do we feel about the Church? As I said at the beginning of this chapter, we do face a challenge, which will find some wonderful positives in the next chapter.

Rhena Taylor was a visionary. Returning from missionary work in Africa, she was unhappy with the way the Church treated those who, like herself, were getting older. Rhena and I chatted about the possibility of an organization to help improve the situation, and I encouraged her, along with several others who believed something could be done, to start up a specifically Christian organization called 'Outlook'. In 1996, Rhena penned this:

> The Western world has been for many years in the grip of ageism, described as 'a deep and profound prejudice against the elderly'. The church has shared in this prejudice. Yes, there is a care line, possibly a lunch club, a friendship club and a weekly meeting for the over-60s in the church, but no one can pretend that church programmes involving older people are high on the list of church priorities, and provision for their spiritual care is often non-existent.[31]

This may be seen as a trifle bitter, but Rhena points out else-where that 'As young people are not the church of tomor-row, neither are older people the church of yesterday.'[32] All churches need to carry a balance that includes young and old and values both. I have a relative whose mother is a member of a church that welcomed a new minster. Soon after arriv-ing, this older lady was talking with the minister's wife, who informed this faithful church member, 'I have no interest in older people whatsoever; I'm only concerned with the youth.' This lady's minister husband is now a bishop. I trust she has changed her attitude and that in her heart she and her hus-band have learned to love the older members of their diocesan flock. If not, they will have big problems with their many rural congregations, almost entirely made up of very elderly people. 'Elders are shown no respect,' written so long ago (Lamentations 5.12) – an attitude still around today.

'Even Christian ministers can be heard complaining about the older members of their congregations and stressing the need for more resources for youth work.'[33]

Arthur Creber is right. He himself was a vicar when he wrote those words. He is backed by the American sociologists Gray and Moburg, who spoke back in the early sixties of 'the neglect of the aged' and an over-emphasis on young people by churches in a society where youth in king.[34] None of these writers is trying to push out the youth in order to accommodate those of older years. But it is a relevant question to ask any church leader, 'How would you like thirty new people in your church?' No leader would refuse such an offer – would they? Advise them that all thirty will be over, say, seventy. What is the reaction? Probably not quite as enthusiastic!

I have enjoyed touring the U.K. to meet many who have moulded my thoughts for this book. Lots of them have given me stories which are enormously positive and which will be shared as we progress through the next few chapters. One, however, stood out as a cautionary tale. It is about a thriving 'daughter' church, formed because the 'mother' church was bursting at the seams some thirty years ago. The main church still thrives but, in a university area, was described to me as 'ninety-five percent students' with a 'rave-style' of service. As you might have realized, I was interviewing an older couple and 'rave' may be their perception of lively worship. The daughter church met in another part of the parish in a school hall with a membership of about ninety, so one would have imagined a happy new vicar, coming to two thriving congregations, with other church plants as well. Alas, no. Within four months, he announced the closure of this congregation, to shocked and stunned silence. The idea was to bring everyone together in one place.

Inevitably, one feels, it had the completely opposite result. A number of the older ones were simply not able to travel: too old to drive and too far to walk. Other older ones toured other local churches to find one which would welcome them and enable them to worship in a way they could cope with. The feeling was that the main church's attitude to these older, faithful worshippers was, 'If you don't like it, go somewhere else.' Of course they took their money with them. This lovely couple with whom I spoke have been able to find a loving fellowship where they once again feel welcomed and appreciated. They simply cannot understand how a minister could come and destroy a close-knit fellowship where so many older people loved the Lord and loved each other. This was not long ago: it had happened only a few months before I met them in late 2017.

I do believe that, if this daughter church had had ninety young people in it, it would never have been closed, but the minister did not want an older congregation or, if he had to have one, it had to be integrated with the young people in the main church. Is this ageism in the church? It looks like it. Perhaps it was partly the fault of the older congregation. As Rob Merchant says:

'An older person's experience of society is too often either taken for granted or considered irrelevant. When the same experience spills over into the Church it is hardly surprising that older members can mount a determined resistance to change, especially if they feel they have been excluded from the process of decision making.'[35]

Whoever was at fault, the result was a tragedy: very few from the daughter church now attend the main church. A fellowship of older worshippers has been broken up, some cannot now make the greater distance each Sunday and some, as my two interviewees reported sadly, are left with watching services and religious programmes on T.V. A rescue act is needed, although now probably too late. There is clearly another side to this story – there always is.

Is it possible for the church to view their older people in the beautiful way God sees them living when he promises the restoration of Jerusalem after the exile? These are lovely words:

'This is what the Lord Almighty says: 'Once again men and women of ripe old age will sit in the streets of Jerusalem, each with cane in hand because of his age. The streets will be filled with girls and boys playing there" (Zechariah 8:4–5)

Perhaps the unpredictability of the weather might need this to have local interpretations! But the kindness to old and young is to be applauded and we need to have both ends of the age ranges in mind in our churches.

Now to our third and final section. A key question for them is how they see themselves in their retirement. We all face the same question.

How we view our ageing

An old song by Eben Rexford[36] has him telling his sweetheart that his older years are clearly visible, with white hairs replacing the brown.

We have already quoted King David's reflection on his own life: 'I was young and now I am old' (Psalms 37.25). He himself was only 70 when he died (2 Samuel 5.4), although this is described as 'having enjoyed long life, wealth and honour' (1 Chronicles 29.28).

Is this how we view our ageing – 'enjoying long life'? Or do we feel more like Pete Townshend of The Who, hoping he would die while he was young?[37]

If this was the hope of Pete Townshend, the song's writer, when he was twenty, he may have to revise his thinking – he is now in his seventies. He will be discovering that, compared with the Swingin' Sixties, 'Old Age is Another Country', as Paige Smith entitles one of her books.[38] Indeed it is. Dr David Field, an Oxford scholar who advised me on this book, listed for me what he calls 'the most common and pressing spiritual and psychological issues of later life.' He includes the following:

- multiple bereavements
- the stripping away of so much which once gave identity – career, phases one and two of parenthood, appearance, possession, recognition
- loneliness
- regret
- despair at being useful
- disproportionate concern with comfort and well-being

- narrowing of horizons
- children who don't believe
- loss of interest in things and appetite for life
- loss of acuity
- unforgiveness
- anger at the world being out of our control

Another friend, who has worked with older people for many years, would add to that long list the doubts, fears and loss of assurance which affect us as we age, especially the fear of being forsaken by God (Psalms 71.18). We can have a preponderance to look back with rose-tinted spectacles at the past, leading to complacency (Ecclesiastes 7.10). I would, sadly, have to add that older age brings its own temptations and sins. The impact of ageing is both individual and personal. Each and every aspect of this long list will not be found in everyone; it is for us to see these as they may be in ourselves and be conscious of the possibilities that they could be in those we would seek to help.

What a lot of challenges later life gives us! If it were not for the African approach that I choose to adopt, I would call these a lot of problems. The consideration of ageing from a personal point of view is, to say the least, not easy. Richard Ford agrees with one of Dr Field's points: 'The world gets smaller and more focussed the longer we stay on it.'[39]

It is no wonder that many do not want to consider themselves as old, and whatever anyone else is doing, they think that they themselves are not ageing. One of the favourite ladies of the entire twentieth century was the wife and then widow of King George VI, the indomitable Queen Elizabeth, the Queen Mother. At a horse race meeting she was heard to say, 'I'd better wander over to see the old people.' She was 96 at the time and clearly was not one of those she was going to see. Mary Thomas wrote an article 'The curse of older age' (quite a title) and said in it,

> If you were to call a thirty five year old man or woman middle aged, you would be considered rude. Call a person over sixty or seventy elderly, what do you mean? I am merely older than someone younger than me.[40]

We want to have long lives, but cannot come to terms with this equating to being old. Long ago, Jonathan Swift put it succinctly: 'Every man desires to live long; but no man would be old.'[41] In all my research, I have been hard pressed to find an older person who admits to being old. This is surely a denial of reality and, even worse, something that will deprive us of the good we can discover in later life. The renowned Swiss psychiatrist Carl Gustav Jung pulled no punches when he said that 'to refuse to grow old is as foolish as to refuse to leave behind one's childhood'.[42] When Paul Tournier wrote his book *Learning to Grow Old*, he made it clear that it was not just for the retired, but also for 'those who are still in the full flood of life', as everyone needs to have a positive view on ageing.[43] As Tournier points out later in that book,

> It is no easy matter to accept that one is growing old, and no one succeeds in doing it without first overcoming his spontaneous refusal. It is difficult, too, to accept

the growing old of someone else, of one's nearest and dearest.[44]

Derek Prime's recent book with the splendid title *A Good Old Age* has a complete section entitled 'Acceptance', which includes the need to 'accept the inescapable indignities and embarrassments of old age', 'the gradual loss of independence in some areas of life', 'the frustrations ageing brings' and 'accepting the changing of times'. He warns against 'pretending old age is not creeping up on us'. Writing in his eighties, these words are from one who is himself old and, therefore, not without experience of this stage of life.[45]

I have to accept this ageing with good grace. When I look back at the lists from Field and Prime of the difficulties we all face, I confess to a sense of fear. I do not go as far as Philip Roth in his pessimistic book *Everyman*, where he bleakly states, 'Old age isn't a battle; old age is a massacre.'[46] He quotes a character whose relative has just died:

Old age is a battle, dear, if not with this, then with that. It's an unrelenting battle, and just when you're at your weakest and least able to call up your old fight.[47]

Surely things are not that bad – but, at least for Roth, they clearly are. Yet even the optimistic Tournier, with all his positivity, has to say, 'In reality, everyone fears old age.'[48] My hope would be that we could be, at least, realistic rather than pessimistic. 'You might feel thirty five,' says Robert McCrum, 'But it makes sense to behave as if you are actually closer to seventy.'[49] I do like another of his comments:

'Sixty, they will say, is the new forty. Actually, sixty is still the old sixty.'[50] He is echoed by comedian Barry Crier: 'I'm fifty nine and people call me middle-aged. How many 118 year old men do you know?'[51]

If we are not careful, all we see are the negatives. We see what we no longer have. Atul Gawande writes,

> It is not death that the very old tell me they fear. It is what happens short of death – losing their hearing, their memory, their best friends, their way of life . . . Old age is a continuous series of losses.

His *Being Mortal* has some cruel, yet honest, comments, this being one of them.[52] He tries to be realistic, as I have suggested, but sets the bar very low:

> The terror of sickness and old age is not merely the terror of the losses one is forced to endure but also the terror of isolation. As people become aware of the finitude of their life, they do not ask for much. They do not seek for more riches. They do not seek more power. They ask only to be permitted, insofar as possible, to keep shaping the story of their life in the world – to make choices and sustain connections to others according to their own priorities.[53]

No wonder my 97-year-old mother- in-law says to me, 'Ian, don't get old. It's not good.' As she sits in her chair, unable to walk more than a few tottering steps, watching the television, reading or doing simple puzzles, she now cannot, in

Gawande's words, shape the story of her life. Good friends have moved away to be nearer their family. She would echo the lament of Dusty Springfield in her song, 'I just don't know what to do with myself', not knowing how to fill her time.[54]

My mother-in-law has the inestimable advantage of a daughter with whom she lives who is a highly qualified nurse who, together with her husband, looks after this very frail member of our family. Both her other daughters visit frequently, as do folk from the church. I am keenly aware of several of my friends who do not have this comfort and security, for whom the sheer loneliness of their later lives is an enormous burden. One of the most poignant things I was told in 2017 was by a remarkable servant of God, who is also a close friend. We will hear of his wife, Liz, when we face the question of our dying, as she died a couple of months before I sat with Cyril, her widower, one Saturday morning in their bungalow in Northern Ireland.

The previous evening I had attended a magnificent 'tribute night' for Liz, to raise money for research into Motor Neurone Disease (from which Liz had died) and to rejoice in the work and life of Liz. More than a thousand had come to hear choirs, soloists and poetry readings. We all sang and rejoiced. How had Cyril felt about the whole event, I asked him. He said how thrilled he had been by the music, by the way his relative, the internationally famous actor Ian McElhinney and his son had read Liz's poems, how a huge amount of money had been raised for such a worthy cause – all so positive. 'But there was just this one thing. When I came home after it was all over, I walked into the empty house and was about to call out to Liz to tell her how great it had been, and. . . .'

Cyril has the great assurance that Liz is safe with the One who has beaten death. This Lord Jesus Christ is with him, too. But the human feeling of lostness and desolation sometimes rears its head, as it had done at that door-opening moment. There are so many who see their ageing in that way: the delicate balance between knowing Christ and never being alone and yet being on their own. I know a single older lady who knows this joy and sorrow, and a man married for many years who is also now a widower. He would be typical of his whole generation which, unlike many who are now younger, relied on his wife for everything and has had to learn to fend for himself. He is often too proud to ask others for the help they would willingly give and, in his lonely existence, he has shrunk back into his shell, a shadow of the man he once was when his wife sustained him. Being a Christian is not the whole answer, although we preach that it is.

It has helped me in writing this book to meet some people who have been up front about how hard they are finding their ageing. So much in the later chapters will be about the wonderfully positive ways many move forward through their older years. I thank God for Gail and her sharing this story. She was only 33 when her husband David died, leaving her with three small children. As they grew, Gail had no time to be lonely, with them and a loving, caring church around her. With great courage, she went forward for ordination and had a happy and successful ministry. Now retired, she has moved north and lives not far from our home. The children are all grown and gone to their own homes, lives and careers.

'I am free to do whatever I like – and I don't know what to do!' Gail is filling her time with what is fun – learning the piano, learning to swim, taking church services. 'But it is being alone that makes me realize I'm lonely,' she told me. 'I've lost my job and my children, I make friends badly, I miss my old church and you have to move away when you retire.' Twelve months after she moved, she felt she was going downhill and went to see the doctor. She told him she had retired, leaving her home, her church and her children. 'No wonder you're depressed!' was his jolly answer!

Gail's loneliness is exacerbated by one particular thing – she misses her grandchildren. She would so love to move near to where at least one of them lives, but house prices further south are prohibitive, and even an extended visit to be with the family simply emphasizes the loneliness on her return north. Time and again as we talked, it was this one word 'loneliness' that kept cropping up. There is no family banter, no energy received from those young and full of it, no sharing each day. 'I'm on my own and, oh my goodness, it's different!'

I have related our conversation in such detail because I am aware of vast numbers who will have a similar story to tell. Ageing for a Christian can be hard. We may view it as a tough call, as Gail does. Paul Simon was a young man when, in his brilliant song 'America', he told his sleeping girlfriend that he had no idea where he was going and how empty he felt inside.[55]

We who have companions in our own homes need to be on the lookout for the Gails of our world – Christians who sit near us in church, who wave across to us after the service. Is it a wave? Stevie Smith's touching little poem, 'Not Waving but Drowning', says she is waving for help and rescue.[56] En passant, it may not have escaped you that one factor in Gail's story is the problem of not being able to move from her modest house in the relatively 'cheap' North East to the vastly more expensive South of England. The Joseph Rowntree Foundation has published a report on poverty, its 2017 findings showing that, since 2012, poverty levels for pensioners have risen to 16 per cent from 13 per cent.[57] For many, loneliness cannot be escaped with the help of a move, because a move cannot be afforded.

Before we fall apart with all this disturbing news, and by way of moving to the many positives that will follow, let me bring some encouraging news: there are many who view their ageing very positively, even proudly. Queen Elizabeth the Queen Mother, whom I quoted earlier, said to her photographer,

> Don't retouch my wrinkles in the photograph. I would not want it to be thought that I had lived for all these years without having anything to show for it.[58]

Getting older, as many will testify, is good. We can view our ageing by looking up, not down. 'Glass half full' is a good expression for those who see their later years as a blessing. In an almost poetic way, in his new book about dying, Robert McCrum says this:

> Among the important lessons about ageing is a new appreciation of simple pleasures: the joy of friendship

and the satisfaction of small victories – an engagement fulfilled or a mundane task completed. Being alive in the world brings its own reward: the wind in your face on a blustery spring day, or the silver-magic of summer moonlight.[59]

He concludes his book with some stirring advice:

Why not celebrate 'nowness'? Discover the joy of wisdom and experience. Cherish your family. Celebrate the human drama in all its variety. Be happy to be old. Feast on the marrow of life while you can. Pass on to fellow survivors, friends and family a positive delight in the world.[60]

As I have explored how ageing is viewed from different standpoints, I have, unashamedly, drawn on many sources to help me. In a chapter full of quotations, here is one with which to close that is seen on many a beautiful poster. It comes from that much-loved writer, C.S. Lewis:

Autumn is really the best of seasons; and I'm not sure that old age isn't the best part of life.[61]

5

Heroes and zeros

My youth was littered with impossible heroes. I watched from the terraces as Jack Charlton rescued Leeds United, but I was unable to kick a ball like that. Tom Graveney came to the Scarborough Cricket Festival and played a cover drive so serenely, as I gazed in wonder. In my growing Christian faith, I was constantly shown the great men and women who were held up as examples that I was supposed to emulate. There were the daring missionaries who went to the Auca Indians in South America and died as they sought to bring the good news of Jesus to this hitherto unknown tribe.

My father was particularly fond of a man called 'Praying Hyde'.[1] He cajoled me and my Christian friends that we should be more concerned with prayer, holding up Hyde as the paragon. This man, my father would tell us, prayed so much that he made grooves on the floor, carved out by his knees as he knelt by his bed. It is true that there was a man called John Hyde, from Illinois in the States, who went out to the Punjab area of India and did pray a great deal, leading to times of wonderful revival. However, the floor of my father's bedroom never had prayer-grooves, and it all made my own prayer life seem continually inadequate.

All this is to make a serious observation: the great heroes of faith, long ago or more recently, can appear so impossible to emulate that we almost give up our own puny efforts.

Books on faith invariably hold up the biblical 'greats' and urge us to copy them, rising to their sublime heights. When we try, we feel we fall backwards and become discouraged. I have to remind myself that Jack Charlton's skills only spurred me on to play better, even though I did not go on to get a World Cup Winner's medal. Tom Graveney made me want to bat with more style, even though I did not even make my school first XI.

To enable each of us in our later years not to lose heart, I am going to take encouragement from some of those in the Bible who, in their own later years, did special things with and for God. I realize I may never reach their summits, but I can still climb my small hill and enjoy the view. As most writers take us on a chronological journey through the Bible, I will take a slightly different approach, as we will now look at what they did, rather than when they did it. Let's meet our heroines and heroes and be stimulated, rather than gaze with despair.

Big work in old age

My wife and I are almost exactly at the age Abraham and his wife were when God called them to make a journey of many hundreds of miles to a new land where, God said, he would make them into 'a great nation' (Gen 12.2). They were 75 and 66 respectively, the sort of age at which most of us are happily slowing down and settling in to a quiet old age. We are not talking about a couple of spring chickens, backpacking on their holiday. This is a completely new beginning, a total leaving of home, neighbourhood, family and friends, taking their nephew, Lot, all their possessions and household and going into the unknown. All this older couple had was an assurance from God:

I will make you into a great nation
And I will bless you;
I will make your names great,
And you will be a blessing.
I will bless those who bless you,
And whoever curses you, I will curse,
And all peoples on earth
Will be blessed through you. (Gen 12:2-3)

And off they went! 'So Abram [as he was then called] left, as the Lord had told him' (v.4). No wonder he has a prominent place among the heroes of faith in Hebrews Chapter 11, where it says that 'By faith Abraham . . . obeyed and went' (Heb 11.8). When we were young, if we were then committed Christians, many of us felt God's call on our lives in one way or another. We did feel led to go for God and looked joyfully into the unknown future, believing in the guidance of the Holy Spirit for the big steps we then took. We are happy to encourage young people today to adopt such an attitude of faith.

God may not call me to such a huge adventure as he did Abraham and Sarah, now I am in my seventies and my wife is in her sixties, but . . . Have I closed my heart to a further call from God now I am Abraham's age? Might it be that God has further plans for me now? Am I open to his call, to his voice speaking to me, to his moving me on?

As if that were not enough, 24 years later it got even more dramatic. After many remarkable events, Abraham is now 99 and his wife 90. Back comes God for a further conversation with his servant, to tell him that he is now Abraham, not Abram, and that he will become 'a father of many nations' (Gen 17.4). He and Sarah are going to have a son (v.16). At their age! No wonder Abraham laughs at the very idea (v.17), as did Sarah (Gen 18.12). The writer to the Hebrews, all those years later, struggles with his own astonishment, describing Abraham 'as good as dead' (Heb 11.12) when this happened. Trying to put this story into our own context, Rob Merchant says this:

> The experience of growing old brings with it for many the reality of physical limitation. However, into this story bursts the actual reality of God's sovereignty over all things, including age, in the question 'Is anything too hard for the Lord?' (Gen 18.14). It is a timely reminder that even when faced with the apparent realities of older age there is still time for God because he is the God of all time and times.[2]

Merchant is right: God can work in our lives whatever our circumstances. The challenge is to be willing for God to have, not just new places, but new plans for our older age. As we all know, the miracle did happen for Sarah and Abraham, with their laughter continuing into the name they called their son: 'Isaac' is from the Hebrew 'one laughs' (Gen 21.3–6).

As if to double the challenge to us to be ready for anything, the Genesis story is all but replicated at the beginning of

Luke's Gospel, where Chapter One has the account of the birth of John the Baptist, a son given to a similarly elderly couple, Zechariah and Elizabeth. The angel Gabriel explains the whole incident in the blunt statement: 'For nothing is impossible for God' (Luke 1.37). Merchant describes these two as 'older rôle models'[3] which is an interesting observation, bearing in mind that Zechariah was so lacking in faith that he was struck dumb (Luke 1.20) from the day he was told what would happen until John was born and given his name (vs.63–64). As I commented elsewhere, 'It is an indication of God's strong approval of older people.'[4]

These two couples, separated by very many years, should not make us feel inadequate by comparison, but encourage us to trust in a God who is not finished doing great, mighty and wonderful things with us and through us, however old we are and however limited we consider ourselves to be.

Things to do

Realistically, not many will be called in the way these four very special ones were. The Bible lowers the bar for others, so we can look at what happens and say, 'Well, I could do that.' Following the Lord is often 'mission possible'. Take Hushai as a start here. He has what one could call a small walk-on part in the conflict between David and his rebellious son Absalom. Reckoned to be 'an old man',[5] David tells Hushai that his going with him would be 'a burden' (2 Samuel 15.33). Perhaps some church leaders today see us older ones in this light. The king is made of finer stuff and sees how his 'friend' (v.37 and 1 Chronicles 27.33) Hushai can not only be of help but be valued as well. David encourages this older man to go as a diplomat and peacemaker, working in Jerusalem to restore order. The wisdom of age can rescue tricky situations. As G.T. Manley observes about Hushai, 'His devotion to his king, and his readiness to undertake a dangerous errand for him, affords a model for the Christian to study and follow.'[6]

There is another side to this story. Viewed from the point of view of Absalom and his fellow conspirator Ahithophel, Hushai would have been seen as a spy and a subversive, coming to ruin their plans and inform David of what was going on – hence Manley's observation that the task was 'dangerous'. This older man needed both wisdom and courage, and so do we, as we work for the kingdom of God. Do we older ones have that courage, to help disasters be avoided in the church, without being seen as those who grumble and complain? We need the wisdom of age to bring about the best result, as Hushai was able to do.

I am so glad to find a couple of grandparents deserving of a mention in the Bible. When Paul writes to his protégé and young Christian leader Timothy, he makes a special mention of where this young man's faith has its beginnings, 'which first lived in your grandmother Lois and in your mother Eunice'. I was blessed in just such a way in my grandmother Anne and my mother, Joan. We Christian grandparents have a special place in our families. I am just sorry that neither grandfather nor father is mentioned!

Lois is following in the beautiful example of an older relative, in the great grandmother of King David, the widow Naomi, mother-in-law of Ruth. The whole book of Ruth is a touching story of family love and how, despite her great and deep sorrows, Naomi is able to bring about the marriage of Ruth to her (Naomi's) relative Boaz. To see how the two women care for each other, support one another in times of sorrow and joy, is to witness intergenerational affection at its best. Rob Merchant writes this:

> The interaction between Naomi and Ruth provides us with a powerful model of how an older woman not only inspired, but in many ways mentored a younger woman. We see Naomi's desire to continue trusting God despite the situation in which she found herself to be, combined with her concern for Ruth and we see Ruth's willingness to be inspired by this older woman in her life. It is a tremendous challenge and encouragement to us today to dare to take on this model.[7]

As I myself have written previously about Naomi,

> She is pictured as a generous, self-sacrificing caring mother-in-law, willing to release her daughter-in-law from any obligations they may have had when her sons died (Ruth 1:8). When Ruth pleaded to stay with her, she took her home, cared for her, and with no small skill led her to long-term happiness. Her self-effacing style is clearly portrayed, but her involvement is held up as an example of how an older woman can be a great influence for good. There is no suggestion that Naomi is either too old, or no longer of any use: the contrary is the case, and the grandson Ruth gave her is said by her neighbours to 'renew your life and sustain you in your old age'

(Ruth 4:15). The whole picture is of an old lady who both gives and receives love as a key figure in the family.[8]

As with all these examples, they are not the only ones in the Bible. No list is exhaustive, but both Lois and Naomi show the place of intergenerational ministry in Biblical times and on into our present day. That is why I have written about grandparents so enthusiastically in other parts of this book.

Moving on or, rather, backwards in the Bible, I find a particular challenge from one of the most positive men you will ever find. He is Caleb. In his forties, we find him standing shoulder to shoulder with Joshua, urging the people of Israel to enter the Promised Land (Numbers 13.30). Forty years later, having finally arrived, there are areas of the country still to conquer. Surely, now, aged 85, it is time to retire? Not a bit of it; Caleb talks with his co-warrior Joshua and explains how he has followed the Lord faithfully and 'wholeheartedly' (Joshua 14.8). He makes this plea:

> So here I am today, eighty-five years old! I am still as strong today as the day Moses sent me out, I'm just as vigorous to go out to battle now as I was then. Now give me this hill country that the Lord promised me that day. You yourself heard then that the Anakites were there and their cities were large and fortified, but, the Lord helping me, I will drive them out just as he said (Joshua 14.10–12).

What could Joshua do but bless this old friend and let him get on with his octogenarian mission? It will come as no surprise that Caleb won through, 'because', as verses 14 and 15 conclude, 'he followed the Lord, the God of Israel, whole-heartedly . . . Then the land had rest.' What a hero! It was Amy Carmichael, the missionary to India, who said, 'I want to die climbing.' Perhaps she had Caleb in mind when she said that, with her other famous comment: 'I would rather burn out than rust out.'[9] Perhaps I should have included Caleb alongside Abraham as one who achieved something mighty in old age, but I could not omit him here.

There are those who do things a little more quietly, but who bless others as they grow older. Only one woman in the Bible is called a 'disciple', a lady called Tabitha, translated as Dorcas (Acts 9.36). She is no Caleb, climbing mountains, but she is wonderful, caring for others who, like herself, struggle with later life. She 'was always doing good and helping the poor.' As Lattimore puts it, 'She was full of good works and the acts of charity which she did.'[10] Her death broke many hearts, resulting in Peter raising her from the dead and restoring her to her ministry of care, making robes and other clothes for widows.

Both Caleb and Dorcas are biblical heroes and challenge us to be active in our service of the God who has not finished with us just because people say, 'How old?!'

The pray-ers

When we come to the specific things we older ones can do, prayer will be right there as a key factor. To set the scene for that, here are a couple of older pray-ers, whose example still glows strongly. The first may be one of the oldest pray-ers in the Bible, so old that the translations are not completely clear how old she really was. Her name is Anna, with just a few verses to her name in Luke 2.36–38. She is either 84 or, in some translations, she has been a widow for 84 years. Luke describes her thus:

> She was very old . . . she never left the temple but worshipped night and day, fasting and praying. (vs.36–37)

Too old to be of any use? If that be so, then prayer is of no use and, after a lifetime of being blessed by the prayers of very old friends of mine, I would have to disagree. Prayer changes things, as a quick sortie back to Exodus will show. There is a battle raging, as Joshua and the Israelite army take on the Amalekites. Moses stands watching the battle from a hilltop. Now in his seventies, he has to let the younger men fight, but still has a vital role to play. The account in Exodus 17.8–13 pictures Moses holding up his arms, clutching 'the staff of God' in his hands. As he holds his hands in prayer to God, so the battle is won. If he lowers his arms, the enemy gains ground. Two other non-combatants, Aaron and Hur, hold Moses' arms and these three older men do spiritual battle, just as Joshua and his men fight physically.

Anna and Moses, two older warriors, both deeply involved in that most vital work of prayer, are an encouragement to all those of us who might be tempted to say, 'There's nothing I can do these days.' These are two of the many men and women in the Bible whose later lives are taken up with prayer. Samuel, as he grew old, is specifically asked by the people to pray for their safety and is able to encourage them as a result (1 Samuel 12.19–23), getting a favourable mention for his being a man of prayer in the Psalms (Psalms 99.6). We are led to believe by those who calculate dates in the Bible that Daniel was probably in his eighties when we read of his adventures in the lions' den. The whole drama unfolded from the fact that he prayed three times a day, getting down on his knees (Daniel 6.10). We will return to this theme again soon.

Use the gift

I want to go back to one of the first heroes I mentioned at the beginning of this chapter, the old father of John the Baptist. Luke says this remarkable thing about him: 'His father Zechariah was filled with the Holy Spirit and prophesied' (Luke 1.67). He then gave the church one of its great songs of worship, often known as 'The Benedictus', in which he spoke, or sang, of the salvation about to be brought through Jesus Christ and that his own son, John, would 'be called a prophet of the Most High' (v.76).

The significance of this for me is twofold: first, that a very old person can be filled with the Holy Spirit, and second, that such a one can exercise a spiritual gift. A similar thing happens in Luke's next chapter, where an old man called Simeon is 'moved by the Spirit' (Luke 2:27), goes to the Temple, meets the infant Jesus and sings his wonderful song, which is commonly known today as the 'Nunc Dimittis' and is sung in churches worldwide. Simeon then blesses Joseph and Mary and prophesies about Jesus and his impact on the world, coupled with the sorrow Mary will have to face.

The third person of note is Anna, recently mentioned, who is described as a 'prophetess' (v.36) who, having met Jesus, prophesies to 'all who were looking forward to the redemption of Jerusalem' (v.38) of 'the child'.

These three, very senior in age, are a big challenge to me. My youthful enthusiasm for the fullness of the Holy Spirit, as we saw many wonders in churches in the 1960s, meant that I enjoyed a life and ministry filled with God's power. I witnessed many who manifested a variety of the Spirit's gifts. Two questions now arise. First, where do we older Christians stand regarding the Holy Spirit in our lives? After all, the words of Joel must surely be for today:

> And afterwards,
> I will pour out my Spirit on all people.
> Your sons and daughters will prophesy,
> Your old men will dream dreams,
> Your young men will see visions.
> Even on my servants, both men and women,
> I will pour out my Spirit in those days.
>
> Joel 2.28–29

Now we have met three older people who are fulfilling this prophecy, which is then taken up and quoted in Peter's famous sermon on the Day of Pentecost, with the same words from Joel, quoted in Acts 2.17–18. David Gooding, commenting on this passage, has this to say:

> The Holy Spirit was offered to all indiscriminately: men and women, young and old, without distinction.[11]

77

To believe that this was only for the short time of the New Testament people and not for us today is to have a limiting view of God: he would do it for them but not for you and me? In my older age, I need more of the fullness of the Holy Spirit, not less than I did when I was younger. In a similar way, second, I need to see that I have a ministry of exercising the gifts of the Spirit that God gives me. If three old people in the Gospel of Luke can have such an impact by their being open to being used by God, ought I not to make myself available to what God might, in his sovereign power, want to do with my later days?

Zechariah, Simeon and Anna send out a clarion call to be filled with, and used by, the Holy Spirit. According to the books of Joel and Acts, we older folk are all in on this. I fear many of us have retreated: the call is here again right now.

The sufferers

One of the many reasons I love the Bible is its honesty in facing the realities of life and not hiding from us that many of the great ones who served God suffered as a consequence. For us older folk, it is a source of comfort to know that we are not unique when it comes to finding the Christian life is pretty tough from time to time. Back in 1987, I collected the Christian writer and speaker Alan Redpath from his retirement flat in Birmingham and drove him to a conference where we were speakers. We got to chatting about our respective lives, and he said how he and his wife were having problems with unkind neighbours. 'Ian,' he said, 'the Christian life doesn't get easier as one gets older.'

A couple of well-known examples from the Scriptures will give credence to this honest assessment. The first is the man whose very name is synonymous with fortitude in really dreadful times, as we speak of 'the patience of Job'. Here is an older man – he has a grown-up family – who is allowed by God to suffer horribly from the loss of property, bereavement of family and personal dereliction of health. Rob Merchant paints the picture:

> Job, an older and respected man, presents us with an image of someone who has walked faithfully during his life and yet is faced with extreme physical suffering. Many of our pioneers of the third age as they journey into their fourth age will be faced with the experience of suffering in their lives.[12]

John Wyatt, in his tour de force *Matters of Life and Death*, comments:

> The book of Job has a great deal to teach us about human suffering. I believe it is particularly relevant in an age which has lost a belief in any positive aspect of suffering. Christians too have been affected by this secular disease. One of the greatest needs of the church today is to rediscover a biblical theology of suffering, and the book of Job is of special significance in this regard.[13]

These two writers – Merchant a theological lecturer, Wyatt a specialist in the medical care of newborn babies, and writing from different perspectives – are united in their high regard for the archetypal sufferer, who shows us how to get through our deep problems and still be able to say words echoed in Handel's Messiah: 'I know that my Redeemer lives' (Job 19.25). Wyatt's whole book deserves a careful reading, where he faces some of life's ultimate problems very directly. After exploring the 'Job' question, he concludes,

> We should learn from the book of Job. There can be no human explanations for the mystery of suffering – only the presence of a loving, suffering and redeeming God.[14]

Job has his 'comforters' who are no comfort at all. Only God can truly understand what this poor man is going through. Sometimes there is no one to whom we can turn as we struggle with our own bereavements, losses and our pain and debilities. Job says, 'Cry to the Lord.' He is right.

My other example is poor old Jeremiah, known as 'the weeping prophet', about whom it has been said, 'It is impossible to plumb the depths of grief into which Jeremiah was plunged.'[15] I once had to write an essay on 'Jeremiah, prophet of doom: discuss' for a theological exam. It was not difficult to agree with the title, although I hope I was able to show how he continually kept his head above water – or sometimes, the mud (Jeremiah 38.6). As a preacher myself, it is occasionally tempting to give up, until I read again Jeremiah's complaint that people 'insult' him and 'reproach' him 'all day long', and yet,

> But if I say 'I will not mention him or speak any more in his name', his word is in my heart like a fire, a fire

shut up in my bones. I am weary from keeping it in; indeed, I cannot.' (Jeremiah 20.8–9).

Into his old age, Jeremiah remained faithful to his calling. As we see him, like Job, rising up to be God's man, we need to have their courage and keep on keeping on.

All the Way

There are many of us who had the great privilege of trusting Christ in our early days. Are we staying the course? In the last two sections of this chapter, I want to look briefly at those who did – and then some who did not. First, the good news: the Bible has many who, by their old age, are still going with and for God. I could have chosen Jeremiah, of course, called as 'a child' (Jeremiah 1.6) and going all the way with God. Instead, I look at Joshua, whose life history spans no less than five Old Testament books. He was a brave young soldier as the people of Israel left Egypt (Exodus 17.10) and the faithful aide to Moses (Exodus 24.13). In his middle age he stood against evil (Numbers 11:28) and led the people into the Promised Land (Numbers 27.18–23).

Then we come to where we read, 'Joshua by then [was] old and well advanced in years' (Joshua 23.1). We gather he was, by then, 110 (Joshua 24.29). How amazing! After serving God right through until that age, he wrapped up his life with this testimony and challenge:

Now fear the Lord and serve him with all faithfulness. Throw away the gods your forefathers worshipped beyond the River and in Egypt, and serve the Lord. But if serving the Lord seems undesirable to you, then choose for yourselves this day whom you will serve, whether the gods your forefathers served beyond the River, or the gods of the Amorites, in whose land you are now living. But as for me and my household, we will serve the Lord (Joshua 24.14–15).

I want to stand up and cheer this fantastic hero! He has made it to the end. Good man!

Samuel was similar. Called by God as a child in the beautiful story of how he heard God's voice in the night (1 Samuel 3.1–10), he went on to anoint David as king (1 Samuel 16.13) and was there at the end, mourned by the whole country (1 Samuel 28.3). I hear of leaders, pastors and priests who either give up or disappear into a very private retirement. They may have good reasons for doing so, but Samuel shows that the priestly anointing is for life. I, for one, want to keep on going in my ministry.

Other examples which come to mind include Israel's greatest king, David. A follower of God as a young shepherd, he did have a famous mid-life crisis but, with God's forgiveness and help, came back to be God's man right to the end of his life. It is touching to see how he handled his failing health and strength. He actually hands the kingdom over to Solomon before he dies, letting Solomon be crowned king while David helps to plan the building of the Temple, which had always been his great longing. The story, in the early chapters of 1 Kings, is a lovely example of how it is possible to lay down many of the burdens of leadership and yet continue to serve God to the very end.

The same could be said of John the apostle, friend of Jesus when he was only a teenager, going on to write his splendid Gospel, and in much later life, penning some beautiful letters and (although some eminent scholars dispute this) finally giving us the Revelation, written possibly in his nineties. John's fellow disciple Simon Peter seems to have written his epistles in his last years. Paul identifies himself as 'an old man' when writing to his friend Philemon (Philemon v.8). (I suppose that is what I am as I have written this!) When one considers all that these people of God went through and then lived on to serve God to their dying days, why should we not emulate them in our day?

From Hero to Zero

Having written already about the honesty of the Bible, I need to conclude this chapter with one or two horror stories, because things do not always work out as they should. Not everyone made it through, and an occasional warning is salutary. I once described this set as 'the not-so-golden oldies'.[16] In these examples, I would not want to suggest that some of these fell away in a final, eternally ruinous sense. Some even get a good mention in the list of heroes cited in Hebrews 11, as with the first one I mention. But they did get it wrong.

It is sad to have to include anyone in this little list, not least because so much had gone well for them in earlier days. They stand as cautionary tales for the best of us. You do not have to go far into the Bible to find one: Noah, commended by all. Genesis introduces him to us with these words:

> Noah found favour in the eyes of the Lord. This is the account of Noah. Noah was a righteous man, blameless among the people of his time, and he walked with God. (Genesis 6.8–9).

Noah finds himself in a very exclusive group, as the writer to the Hebrews includes him among those singled out who lived 'by faith'.

> By faith Noah, when warned about things not yet seen, in holy fear built an ark to save his family. By faith he condemned the world and became heir of the righteousness that comes by faith. (Hebrews 11.7).

Everyone loves the way God established his covenant with Noah that the world would never suffer another overwhelming flood by giving the sign of the rainbow (Genesis 9.13). If the story could have ended there, it would have been perfect. Fairy stories end like that, with the rainbow's multi-colours and all at peace. The Bible is not a fairy story so, alas, we get the whole truth, which shows an old man getting drunk and making a fool of himself (Genesis 9.20–23). It is not a pretty picture, nor a happy end to a long life lived in exceptional service of God. In mitigation (I used to be a Solicitor, pleading for people in court), some commentators advise that we do not blame Noah too much. Derek Kidner writes of Noah's 'inexperience' of the effect of fermented grapes[17], while D.F. Payne points out that

'Noah's drunkenness is not openly reproved, and it may be due to ignorance of the potency of wine; he was the first to attempt viniculture.'[18] He was able to speak out prophetically after the event. But it is not the way one would wish to go.

Then there is Rebekah, wife of Isaac and mother of Esau and Jacob. Hers is the story of a woman who had a good relationship with God and was used to praying and receiving answers. We read that 'She went to enquire of the Lord' (Genesis 25.22). The story of her romance in Genesis 24 is delightful, two young people who trusted God and came together in a deep and lasting love. Seemingly unable to have children, they made it a matter of prayer and were blessed (Genesis 25.21). But, as the boys became older and Rebekah aged, she sided with one of her sons to the detriment of the other, with antagonism and deceit, leading to a division which lasts up to today. Her favoured son, Isaac, had to run away from home, and the animosity never really healed. God had to work despite Rebekah rather than with her. She could have been a fine godly parent. How we need wisdom in our older lives as we seek to be good family members. If Rebekah could get it wrong, so can we. God help us to get it right.

For those of us in any kind of leadership or ministry, Eli's story is a warning that the very top people can fail. This was the man who sided with his wicked sons Hophni and Phinehas, allowing them to commit many evils, instead of rebuking them and standing up for God's ways. The whole story, in the opening chapters of 1 Samuel, is of a man who is aware of God at work, giving good advice to young Samuel when God calls the boy (1 Samuel 3.8–9). His tragic end, as he falls and breaks his neck, does not make good reading (1 Samuel 4.18) for a man who 'led Israel for forty years'. It is always a tension whether we make God number one in our lives, especially if our family is not 'with us' in this. Even the top leaders in our churches can fail: they need our support and prayers.

I am not anxious to dwell on the so called 'failures', so just one more: the tragedy of Israel's first king, the disastrous Saul. 'There is no-one like him among all the people,' Samuel had to say (1 Samuel 10.24). With every opportunity to get it right, his life seemed to go on a never-ending spiral downwards, with his own words being 'I have sinned' (1 Samuel 15.24) and, in old age, 'I have acted like a fool and have erred greatly' (1 Samuel 26.21). This is not Saul, the fine young king; this is a man who is nearly seventy years old. One of the most popular songs played at funerals is Frank Sinatra's 'I did it my way'[19]. That is not the way. Saul could have gone with God, but he chose to be his own man and he died on his own sword in battle (1 Samuel 31.5). Frank Sinatra's own last words are reported as being, 'I'm losing,' as he died in May 1988. They could have been Saul's. The lesson is there: stay close to God as you age.

The expression 'Hero to Zero', now so popular, speaks for itself. I do not want it inscribed on my tombstone.

A later hero

Ten years before his death, John Wesley wrote this: 'I have lived this day fourscore years: God grant that I may never live to be useless!'[20]

Zero or Hero? Let us now find how we ourselves can get it right.

6
To be or . . .

> To be or not to be, that is the question:
> Whether 'tis nobler in the mind to suffer
> The slings and arrows of outrageous fortune,
> Or to take arms against a sea of troubles
> And by opposing end them.[1]

Here he is again, the man who plagued our lives as some of us suffered his works during our 'O' and 'A' level English studies. As I now move into what it means to be retired, William Shakespeare poses two key questions for this vital subject. The first is, is it all worth it? Are we going to get older and retire, or shall we simply give up? To save us going down what could be a road of despair, let me reassure you that I am about to give very many reasons why we should go on and not quit.

There is another, less obvious question that could be read into what Shakespeare makes Hamlet say in his most famous and much quoted soliloquy. We have spent our lives thus far primarily 'doing'. Our frenetic society has had us working, often very hard, giving us too little space for anything else. Now we come to retire, what are we to do now? I want to suggest that this should not be the first question. Hamlet may be asking whether he should live on or not, but his words begin by using some words that, though vitally significant, can be lost in this speech. Those words are, 'To be or not to be'. Are we going to spend the rest of our lives carrying on the same as we always have, or are we going to make a sea-change and discover the joy of 'being', as well as 'doing'? The purist will challenge my misquoting Shakespeare, and I realize he is having Hamlet make the choice between life and death, rather than being and doing, but I have chosen this famous quotation to make my point.

We live in a media-dominated era, when our thinking is done for us. When René Descartes wrote 'Cogito ergo sum' (I think, therefore I am),[2] he had not envisaged a time when this would become 'Tesco ergo sum' (I shop, therefore I am!) One of the wonderful delights of getting older is being able to have time to 'smell the roses' (as former Pink Floyd member Roger Waters sings on his recent album 'Is this the life we really want?' – a challenging question in itself[3]), to take life a little easier, to 'rest beside the weary road and hear the angels sing'.[4]

I have every intention of looking at what we can 'do' in Chapter 7. But before we rush headlong into another round of activities to replace the ones we lay down on our retirement, I believe it essential to look first at how we can answer Hamlet with the response that we will, indeed, 'be'. Let me suggest four areas that deserve our serious consideration, so we give Shakespeare a good run for his money.

To be at peace

On the mountain road (the A83) between Loch Lomond and Loch Fyne, in the west of Scotland, where Glen Croe meets Glen Kinglas, there is a little hollow with the beguiling name 'Rest and be thankful'. It actually says that on the map. What a shame to ignore its invitation and rush on, missing the glorious panoramic views, as well as the rest itself. I confess I have often driven along and failed to stop there, hoping for even better views ahead, but missing the one right there on the road beside me.

I am also ashamed to say that much of my life has been lived like that. Often I have fallen into the trap of the term used by Weber, 'the Protestant Work Ethic',[5] whereby we all have to work our little socks off to somehow be acceptable to God and 'prove' our faith is real. How often I have forgotten, or ignored, the beautiful words of Hebrews 4: 9–10:

> There remains, then, a Sabbath-rest for the people of God: for anyone who enters God's rest also rests from his own work, just as God did from his. Let us, therefore, make every effort to enter that rest, so that no-one will fall by following their example of disobedience.

The danger is of seeing God's 'Sabbath-rest' as something only for the future, when we die and enter glory. Even a cursory glance will show that the verbs are all in the present tense. Of course, we will rest when we die. Yet, as David Gooding makes clear in his commentary on these verses, they are for the here and now as well as the there and then. As he argues, we are still in the fight against evil, but 'that does not mean that we have to wait until we die or until the Lord comes before we can begin to enjoy our heavenly inheritance.'[6] As we get older, we need to beware of assuming that our rest is only a future hope, so failing to enter that rest now.

It is a balance. As Dr Garry Williams has said to me, 'Some are frenetic and don't know how to rest, but some are self-indulgent and stop serving.' I am not going to suggest we stop serving God; a whole chapter follows with positive ideas. But I do not want to echo Sir David Attenborough, where the Times said of him, 'The 91-year-old broadcaster and naturalist said that the thought of not working filled him with dread.'[7] Sometimes we have to lay down our life's work and realize things have to stop. I spoke with Elizabeth Stacey about the very positive progression made when the closing came for the Outlook Trust, founded a number of years ago by Rena Taylor to help reach out with the Gospel to older people.

'It had served its purpose,' Elizabeth, one of its leaders, told me. 'Other organizations have grown up to do the work we were doing. We tried everything to continue, but we could not find new Trustees, our Chairman fell ill, and although we were sad to see it close, we felt that was how God was leading us.' I have seen too many Christian organizations go on beyond their 'sell-by date' not seeing the wisdom of Elizabeth's words. Faith in Later Life, which has sponsored the writing of this book, was partly launched with the residual assets from Outlook, giving its work a natural progression into a positive future venture. What is true for Outlook may also be true for our own lives. We have to learn to rest and be at peace with that decision. That peace comes through having peace with God – the second 'To be'.

To be with God

'Therefore, since we have been justified through faith, we have peace with God through our Lord Jesus Christ' (Romans 5.1). 'Rest' and 'peace' are from God, who gives them to us through Jesus who loves us. Roger Hitchings, when giving lectures on this subject, points out how later life is honoured by God, describing Himself as 'the Ancient of Days', while 'the hair on his head was white like wool' (Daniel 7.9). Hitchings goes on to show how age and wisdom are often put together in the Bible (Proverbs 4.1–9, 16.31, 20.29).

Because God himself understands the word 'old', it must be central to our lives to simply 'be' with Him. How can we do this? We need to obey the injunction, 'Be still, and know that I am God' (Psalm 46.10). Here is the call to 'practice the presence of God', the title of a book written after his death about Brother Lawrence, who lived from c.1614 to 1691. He was, as a youth, in a wood and realized God was there. 'If God is here,' he told himself, 'then he is everywhere – so I can never be out of his presence.' He practised this truth throughout his life. He never achieved either fame or position; his main tasks were washing up in the kitchen and, in later life, repairing sandals. He exhibited a profound peace, so that many came to him for help and guidance. His anonymous biographer gathered his conversations and letters into the small but wonderful book *The Practice of the Presence of God*.[8] Could there be a greater testimony to 'being' with God throughout our lives and especially as we grow physically more tired? His full title as a monk was 'Lawrence of the Resurrection' – so beautiful.[9]

The great thing about this is that, in allowing ourselves to 'be' with God, we are not alone. He has said, 'Never will I leave you, never will I forsake you' (Hebrews 13.5). Philip Roth, in his book *Everyman*, writes of one of his central characters:

> He had chosen to live alone, but not unbearably alone.
> The worst of being unbearably alone was that you had
> to bear it – either that or you were sunk.[10]

What a contrast with God's promise to always be there. What an encouragement for us to have an intimate, moment by moment relationship, which is especially seen in two ways. The first is in a life of prayer. I agree with Derek Prime, who in his A to Z book on how to love and follow Jesus in later years includes 'I is for Intercesson'.[11] He urges that we pray constantly for others, and he is right. Throughout my ministry as an evangelist, I have had the most faithful people who have prayed for me and my work. I spoke at the funeral of one of these folk, a very old lady whose life was one of deep intercessory prayer, and said how I now needed to find 20 new prayer partners to replace her!

My older friend John is like that. He has problems walking, so he is at home a lot. A few days before I was due to fly to Tanzania in January 2018, he phoned me to say, 'I've got your schedule and I'm praying for you each step of the way.' Then, with less than 24 hours before the flight, he called again with these words: 'I've seen the terrible snow forecast, old man. Are you still going?' Confirming that I was, he responded, 'I'll be having a word with Father for your safety – and that you'll be on time for your connection.' John is a man who has been frenetically busy in industry, even being awarded the M.B.E. for his services. But now, he has learned to be still with God and 'faithful in prayer' (Romans 12.12). What a friend – and what a blessing! I can only testify that his prayers were answered in truly remarkable ways.

Having said all this, I would still want to go back to Brother Lawrence. Prayer must be more than just intercession; it has to be a deep and intimate relationship with our Father God, who wants us simply to be his children, enjoying the silences as well as the conversations, the ordinary chats as well as the glory times. A walk will not have unending chatter; it will have many silences, even when with friends on the same path. So it should be in our walk with God, so that our lives and prayers intermingle.

Which leads to letting God 'be' there for us. Our older years give us a new opportunity to get into our Bibles and let God speak to us through its pages. This must mean more than the old joke about the child seeing Granny reading her Bible and telling her friend that she was revising for her final exams!

Speaking of which, a friend called Brenda gave me a great story as I was writing this. I had said to her that, in a sermon early in 2018, the preacher had admitted, rather sadly I felt, that 'Revelation is a closed book to me.' I should have invited him to the little home group my wife and I host each Monday, where we have been revelling in this exciting book week by week, with some help from the guides provided by Tom Wright.[12] My friend, Brenda, had gone upstairs one day to where her mother, Elsie, was in bed, nearing the end of her life. Elsie was reading Revelation, and Brenda asked why she was doing this, it being such a hard book to understand. Elsie's reply was a classic: 'You don't book an exotic holiday without reading the brochure'![13]

Some of the great leaders of the church of long ago, among them Origen, Ambrose and Benedict, have given us the suggested practice of 'Lectio Divina' (Latin for 'Divine Reading'). This is a way to gently meditate on God's Word, rather than rushing through it. Lectio Divina involves reading a passage, meditating on it, praying and then contemplating on the Word. We who may hold a distinctive style of churchmanship do need to be careful that we do not reject excellent ideas because they seem to originate in styles which are 'not us'. I have already quoted 'Be still'; this is a way to be still as we let God's voice whisper his Word into our hearts.

This is all a way of being able, as Billy Graham encourages us, to 'see your retirement as a gift from God.'[14] We can actually move forward in what is called 'cognitive ageing', where we improve in our wisdom and experience, even if we struggle with our memories.[15] Graham puts it well:

You may still be an active senior adult, or you may be riddled with aches and confined to bed, but you can still be a productive servant of Jesus Christ by filling your mind with the knowledge of Jesus Christ and, as Peter did, impact those around you with hope: 'In keeping with his [Christ's] promise we are looking forward to a new heaven . . . So then, dear friends . . . grow in the

grace and knowledge of our Lord and Saviour Jesus
Christ (2 Peter 3.13, 14, 18)[16]

It will give us the greatest joy, as our lives age, to 'be' with
God as we go along. Here is what Derek Prime enjoins and
with which I agree:

> Old age is a time when we have to give up things. We
> cannot do as we once did things that require a lot
> of physical energy, like running or jumping. Even
> walking may be limited and sometimes a problem. We
> have to give up holding positions of responsibility in
> the community or our church fellowship. We have to
> let go and not hold on to things that ought to be given
> up. But there is one thing we can do until our dying
> days: we can pursue godliness (1 Timothy 6.11)[17]

And now – let's look at how we can be a blessing to those
around us, as we look at those with whom we come into
contact.

To be with others

In Alnmouth, on the Northumberland coast, near where
I live, is an Anglican friary. Its chapel has one of the most
stunning views you will ever see, overlooking, from its el-
evated position, the North Sea rolling in as it reaches gold-
en sands. It is a place of retreat for Christians from many
denominations, where lives are restored. It is cared for by
men of God who dress simply in brown habits and sandals.

When my wife and I arrived up here in 2006, we had the joy of meeting its oldest resident, Brother Edward. Right up to his death, not long ago, he was much loved, not only in the worship, but by his being there.

Every morning, except on very inclement days, Brother Edward would go down the steep drive and along the road into the village to get his paper. And then, instead of wandering back to the friary, he would sit down on a bench beside the only main road through the village and read the paper as if he nothing better to do. Few knew his family background, son of an important man in London. They only saw an elderly soul, wearing distinctive garb. Though few knew of his former life, yet many would not only see him, but drift over and join him on that bench. What conversations then took place! Sometimes it became almost like a confessional. The lonely, the lost, the wanderers, the wonderers – they all met with a man of God. Brother Edward had that remarkable gift, the art of Presence, of being there and being a friend to each and every passerby, whether a local from the village or a holiday maker from afar.

I am happy to have been one of those, although my meetings with Edward were in the comfort of an armchair by the fire in the friary. He was a true counsellor. Even more, he was a holy example of giving time to those who needed friendship, counsel and encouragement. There is no park bench on the way to the shop in my nearby village when I make a similar walk up the road to get my morning paper. But I am now in the habit (no pun intended!) of being the one who greets those who are on a similar newspaper quest, to wave to each motorist as they rush off to work, and to make time to greet and exchange a word with the person behind the counter and anyone who seems to need a word of encouragement. It is said that many never speak to anyone else in an entire day. I know one man who cares for his very disabled wife and only gets out as he rides his bike for his paper. I would be ashamed if I was so busy that I could not have a couple of minutes to lift his day. Brother Edward is a gentle reminder that I should do this, and it is such a joy.

Paul Tournier writes of how vital this is for our lives: 'the restoration to our impersonal society of the human warmth, the soul that it lacks'. He challenges us with these words:

> It is a civilisation based on the sense of the person that I pray for. For it is not in the least necessary to reject our society and its benefits. What we must do is to introduce a personal relationship between man and man into the very heart of this society . . . we need . . . men who see the contrast between the wealth of our technological progress and the poverty of our personal relationships, and who will try to improve the latter. Now this is where I see that the old have a real job to do.[18]

How can we do this as we seek to be friends? We can be a listening ear for others who, possibly like us, find this getting older not at all easy. I do commend Billy Graham's book *Nearing Home*. It is much more intensely personal than much of his previous writings, good though they are. He opens with these words:

I never thought I would live to be this old.

All my life I was taught how to die as a Christian, but no one ever taught me how I ought to live in the years before I die. I wish they had because I am an old man now, and believe me, it's not easy.

Whoever first said it was right: old age is not for sissies. Get any group of older people together, and I can almost guarantee what their favourite topic of conversation will be: their latest aches and pains.[19]

For Graham, with his enthusiastic preaching over the years, this is a new style and a very honest and personal one at that. Good for him! I find it significant that, within a paragraph, he has introduced personal relationships and the sort of conversations we have. A quick flip through an address or personal phone book will throw up the names of those who need to talk in this way. I have done this and now have a list of good friends who need a regular call. One has lost her husband after dementia, another has seen his wife die from a horrible, debilitating disease, a third is a lifelong bachelor living alone – the list goes on. Every month I give each and every one a call, to see how they are and assure them of my love and prayers.

It is not surprising that Billy Graham devoted part of his book to the value of friendship, telling his readers to 'remember your friends'. He urges that they 'tell them you care', that they 'keep in touch', as well as 'pray for them'.[20] It is a poor argument to say that these friends should phone me, although some do. That is no reason for not taking the initiative and if, as Graham says, they have to talk about 'their latest aches and pains', then so be it. My experience is that, if I am positive, my friends react in the same way.

I would urge a further step here, in our being friends, which is to make contact with others to thank them as you look back over your life. In 1 Thessalonians 5.18, Paul says that we are to 'Give thanks in all circumstances, for this is God's will for you in Christ Jesus.' A few years ago, I felt a clear nudge from the Holy Spirit to put this into practice in a rather special way. I sat down and thought through all the people who had been a blessing in my life, from my early days right up to the present time. Clearly, some – like my mother, who died when I was 22 – were no longer with us. For these members of the 'church triumphant' I simply gave thanks to God. But there were many still around. The list of the living came to 53.

Out came paper and pen, envelopes and stamps, and slowly but surely I got down to writing to each and every one. There was Norman, whose story is elsewhere in this book, who had been my Bible Class leader in my young teens and who never gave up on me. There was Herbert, the wise leader of the Youth Camp where, in my twenties, he invited me to be the padre and to share the Good News of Jesus with many young lads, some of whom became real Christians during those long ago summers by the Cornish seacoast. He put up with so much from a raw new evange-list, but his patience and words of wisdom helped to mould my ministry. And there was my uncle, who took me to see 'Bambi' when I was a little boy.

There had to be some hunting for current addresses, but I got there. I made each letter unique and full of gratitude. A number replied generously, but that was not the point of my writing, nor of my putting what I did in this book. I really did want to say 'thank you', and I really want to encourage my readers to do the same. I know how much this means, because once in a while I get such a letter. Rachel wrote to me not long ago, having hunted for my address. She related how she had come to a morning service when a young girl and I had preached at her village church. At the end she had prayed to trust Christ. All these years later, she recalled my running to my car to get her a special booklet I had written for children. Now she wanted to thank me. You may imagine the joy in my heart as I read her letter. I knew, once again, how glad I was that, in my later years, I had written that sort of letter myself.

I was waiting for a plane in Tanzania in January 2018. Into the departure lounge came a husband and wife, dressed splendidly in short sleeved white shirts, he in black trousers and she in a black skirt, the shirts emblazoned with the symbols of the Salvation Army. They were clearly leaders in that part of the country. I wandered over to where they were sitting and introduced myself. I told them how, as a boy, I had stood listening to a Salvation Army band in my home town. A youngster in a Salvation Army bonnet had introduced a hymn, saying the words, 'You need Jesus to be your Saviour.' The words had touched my heart and, that evening, I did trust Jesus. When I told this couple, they were overjoyed with my renewed thanks to them for their present-day faithfulness. Surely a word of thanks is for old friends – and for new ones. I made friends that day.

To be happy

I am having to tread carefully here. In talking with others about what I intended to write about, I used the expression, a 'bucket list'. I was interested in the reaction I got. One said (I will not name names), 'It is good to enjoy what God has made and we can be almost Gnostic in our unease about it. At the same time, we are still, in retirement, to seek first God's kingdom and his righteousness.' I take the point, and I hope my desire to put God first comes through clearly in all this book's pages.

However, I am encouraged by the psalmist when he says of God, 'He will give you the desires of your heart, as you delight yourself in the Lord.' (Psalms 37.4). Being happy is not, as another has warned, 'working backwards from the world's estimate of what life is all about rather than working forwards from what we know of God's calling and gifts'. I do not disagree with these sentiments, but my reading of the Scriptures and my experience of being a Christian would take me to a place where my Heavenly Father wants me to enjoy the good things in life, as long as I can do that with a clear conscience. I am with Billy Graham once more on this:

Does this mean it is wrong to relax and enjoy life during our retirement years? No, not at all; to say this would be to say that God doesn't want us to enjoy the good things He gives us – which isn't true. The writer of Ecclesiastes said, 'However many years a man may live, let him enjoy them all' (11.8). The apostle Paul repeated the Old Testament's command for children to honour their parents, so that 'you may enjoy long life on the earth' (Ephesians 6.3). God knows that we need rest and exercise and relaxation; after a gruelling period of ministry, Jesus urged his disciples to 'come with me by yourselves to a quiet place and get some rest' (Mark 6.31).[21]

Along with my advisors, Graham immediately says that, if our only goals in retirement are to have as good a time as possible, then we may have fallen into a trap of empty, meaningless activity. They are all quite right. I go with Clifford Pond, whose book *Autumn Gold* has, as its subtitle, *Enjoying Old Age*. He says this, in a chapter headed 'Relax!':

Sometimes there are circumstances such as ill health, that take the shine off the benefits of retirement and make it less enjoyable. But what a blessing it is when the pressures of paid employment are lifted! What a joy now to spend more time with a partner or friends, to stay in bed a little longer, have an after dinner nap (if you like that sort of thing!) or to develop an interest or hobby that has been, perforce, neglected until now.[22]

Let me suggest, first, that we go back to what was said in the last section and reconsider our friends. A few years ago, I heard that a man who had been very influential in my ministry in Northern Ireland was retiring and that his farewell service would be on a certain Sunday. I agreed with my wife that, if I had heard that he had died, I would doubtless go to his funeral. The obvious was staring us in the face – why not go to celebrate his life when he and I could meet, greet and share fellowship once more? The look of total joy which spread across his face when he saw me on this last Sunday in his church made the flight and time totally worthwhile. There was such happiness.

In a similar vein, my wife and I went to the other end of England to see Norman, the Bible Class leader I have already mentioned, where he sat in a nursing home, aged 92. In my own retirement I now had the time and energy to drive down hundreds of miles to find enormous happiness in renewed face to face fellowship. I find it remarkable to read what Jesus did when he rose from the dead. No great crowds, no grand parade; instead, he met with the ones and twos – Mary Magdalene, Peter, the two going to Emmaus, ten here and eleven there. He made individuals happy.

I think I have my critics onside so far. Now let me push the boat out a little – literally, in one case. These two examples are, unashamedly, 'bucket lists'. My wife has been nothing short of amazing in my life and in my ministry. Our entire courtship was spent saying 'Hello – Goodbye' as I toured the country as a youth evangelist, popping in to see her and then off again to some far-flung part of the UK. After nine years of our marriage, during which I worked as a solicitor, God called us to a new time as an evangelist and wife. We had four sons, and Ruth did the majority of bringing them up, resolving not to have a career until all had left home.

After 25 years of this, it was surely her turn. Her faithfulness to God and to me had been (and continues to be) extraordinary. I asked Ruth what she would like to do most in the world, before the term 'bucket list' came into vogue.

She replied that she would like to see the whales off Alaska. I was shocked. For someone who hated flying and sailing, it seemed ridiculous, and I told her so. 'I want to see the whales off Alaska,' came the reply. To cut a long story short, off we went. On the very day of our silver wedding anniversary, our cruise liner docked at an Alaskan port. On the 'to do' list that day was the chance to take a small, local boat to go 'whale watching'. Naturally we went. After half an hour, our local guide spoke to us in hushed tones. 'In over ten years of taking people out like this,' he said, 'I have never seen so many whales so close to this boat as we are seeing now. You are so lucky.'

No, skipper, we were not 'lucky'. We were being given a unique gift for my longsuffering wife, as whales' tails rose and fell. God loved his daughter that day as he honoured her for being the powerhouse behind a roving evangelist. Even a glorious black and white orca hove into view, as the killer whale showed how friendly he could be. If that's a 'bucket list', then I, for one, am for it.

My own 'bucket list' was actually Ruth's idea. In 2011, I mentioned over the breakfast table on January 1st that this was a special year for me. It would be the sixtieth anniversary of my becoming a Christian and the fiftieth year of my preaching. 'We have to celebrate!' was Ruth's immediate and enthusiastic reply. 'What would you like to do?' To both our surprise, I came up with a very strange answer. 'I'd like to go to Geneva, to see where John Knox (my ancestor) met John Calvin and helped to forge the Reformation.' With no idea of the weather, we flew out at the time of my own birthday – February. The temperature in the Geneva area never got above minus ten Celsius. Lake Geneva's shores were splendidly iced over. But we got to see the very church where these great leaders met and ministered and, like a good tourist, I had my photo taken beside the enormous mural alongside my namesake. 'Bucket list'? Yes, sir!

In each of these two personal examples, God certainly did give us the desires of our hearts. I am not ashamed to say that there are one or two items on our bucket lists still to be fulfilled. Happiness is from God and we are grateful for his generosity.

Inevitably, the 'be' and 'do' of retirement overlap, and we are already into some 'doing', but two of my friends show how the two can fit together. The first is Keith, who retired as vice-principal of a sixth form college aged 60 and is now 84, having taught there for 33 years. He is still very active. He and his wife were the force behind the founding of a Christian care home, he as chair of trustees, she as matron. He told me that, now much older, he has resigned as chair and become Director of Gardening! In his eighties, he visits for the church, helps run Alpha courses, leads people to Christ and has struggled with the loneliness of widower-hood after his wife, Olive, died of cancer seven years ago. He is especially used by God to get alongside those who struggle with life, whether they are depressed or learning to recover after divorce.

In chatting with Keith, the thing I realized was how he has changed since I first met him over 35 years ago. He was always as he is now, a do-er. But he is a new man today. He speaks today of his need for an inward life with the Lord. He admits to having grown more spiritually in the last three years than at any other time in his life. I repeat, Keith is in his eighties. Here is what he said: 'I now see myself as I am. Before, I had no time for myself, but, now I'm single, I have time to be with the Lord. I get up at seven-thirty. I sit in my armchair, and I hear God tell me that, when I confess my sins, I am forgiven straightaway. I had always felt I had to be good for a while, but the Lord is teaching me new things. The Lord is doing something in my inner life, even though I still "do" many things.' He has learned to 'be' in his life, and Keith is a new man in old age.

The day after chatting with Keith (in February 2018), I enjoyed a coffee with Sue, now 92. Sue's husband, Gavin, died when she was 60. She told me how she went 'a bit mental' as a result, saying he was like a tree and she was the branch, so she was lost without her tree. Her church surrounded her with prayer in her brokenness, and God gave her a new life. But like Keith, God is working in her right now. 'My faith has grown more and more in the last year,' she enthused. Imagine – she is in her nineties.

I asked her how this was possible. 'I wake up every morning with the thought, "oh, another day," and I could be so negative. At that moment I read a little book with three positive verses from the Bible and then get up. After breakfast I read *Every Day with Jesus*'. Sue is pleased that 'I have all my marbles.' Despite her age, she still leads two prayer groups and helps with Bible studies. She has a group of ladies who started meeting with her when their children were babies, and 'now they are all at university,' but they still come in their fifties to meet with Sue, their leader. She is a keen member of her church. 'I don't always agree with the clergy (her husband was one, her son was a bishop), but the church is my family and they love the Lord. If I disagree, I keep quiet about it!'

Sue's secret is, once again, simple. In all the things she 'does', she has learned to 'be'. 'God gives me enthusiasm,' she told me. 'Every day I get re-converted. Every day I read my Bible. I start each day giving myself to God, and I don't worry about next week, whether my teeth will fall out or the car will rust. I say to myself, "You've only got today to live for God." It is the Lord who has held me, not me who has held the Lord.'

As you will guess, I came away from my coffee time with Sue inspired and challenged. In all my 'doing', I need to learn again how 'to be', as the Bard of Avon once said. As we now come to the 'doing', may we know that we are human 'beings' first of all.

7

Not retired – refired!

Picture the scene. We are in a cellar in a suburb of Madrid, in the midst of the Spanish Civil War. We are with a group of soldiers about to go on a raid, up the steps and into the street, to attack a building on the other side of the road. The captain speaks to his men and tells them that he and the sergeant will lead the raid. There will be no support, and the enemy is waiting for them. Those who go first will certainly die.

Antoine de Saint-Exupéry, whom we have met already in a previous story from his masterpiece *Winds, Sand and Stars*, is actually in the room at the time, where the sergeant drinks some brandy and falls asleep, a man about to die. The telephone rings, just before the time they are meant to go, with the news that the attack is off. Exupéry relates how he stares at this soldier, now reprieved. Without speaking to the man, he asks this silent question: 'Sergeant, Sergeant, what will you do with this gift of life?'[1]

I have told this story to highlight that question: what are we, who have been spared to live right now, going to do with our gift of life? It is time to think through what we can do to maximize the days, months and years that may lie ahead of us. The heading for this chapter comes courtesy of my friend Ken Clarke, retired Bishop of Kilmore, Elphin and Ardagh in the Church of Ireland. We met in late 2017, and I told him about this book on retirement. 'No, Ian,' he told me, in his refreshingly enthusiastic style, 'Not retired – refired!' He even wears a badge with a flame on it and the one word 'Refired'. How can we live, and be refired?

Let me set the benchmark high. Dr Jim Packer, whose writings have blessed many over the years, has written a lovely little book entitled *Finishing Our Course with Joy*, subtitled *Ageing with Hope*. In his eighties, he says this:

> Some grow old gracefully, meaning fully in the grip of the grace of God. Increasingly they display a well-developed understanding with a well-formed character: firm, resilient and unyielding, with an unfailing sense of proportion and abundant resources for upholding and mentoring others. . . . Glorifying God should be our constant goal.[2]

This is some challenge – and so is the following, although no one knows who said it. It is often, mistakenly, attributed to John Wesley, but researchers deny this. But here it is anyway!

> Do all the good you can.
> By all the means you can.
> In all the ways you can.
> In all the places you can.
> At all the times you can.
> To all the people you can.
> As long as ever you can.

With these challenges from Packer and Anon., let's see what we can do. But, first:

Don't do nothing

We are living in a longevity revolution. No previous generation has had so many who have lived so long. We are pioneers, and like many who have set out on journeys into the unknown, we can simply freeze in our tracks, not knowing where to go or what to do. No one can tell us exactly how to be retired, as each one of us is unique. Doing nothing is clearly a possibility, but one to be avoided at all costs. It will quickly destroy us from sheer boredom.

> Lots of retired people are bored because they do not know what to do with their enforced liberty! For lack of imagination, lack of habit, lack of training, they let themselves go, and take no interest in anything. They retire into a shell of boredom, and in the end renewal becomes impossible, and they become a burden to others. But the germ of this passivity has been there within them for years. They have not realized it, because the routine of work and social life has covered up the void in their personal lives. So many people – including young people – claim liberty, and they have little idea of what to do with it when they get it, because they have not prepared for it. We have been trained for work and not for leisure.[3]

These are strong words from the medical doctor Paul Tournier. Ageing is not just about decline and loss; it is part of creation. We need a big canvas for our lives, to include productive activity in our later years. We need to prepare well and get on with it.

Make plans

'Don't retire, re-tyre.' Everyone seems to have a new slant on the word and this one comes courtesy of Roger Hitchings, in conversation in January 2018. As we may pop on a set of winter tyres to travel more safely in inclement weather, so we need to get re-tyred for our journey into challenging times ahead in our later lives. In their rather scarily titled book, *The 100-Year Life*, Lynda Gratton and Andrew Scott tell us, 'We all have to actively think about our future and begin to sketch a pathway that works for us.'[4] The implication here is that this needs to be done whatever our current age. Some of the great Christian leaders also urge this course of action. While Gratton and Scott's book is wholly secular, their advice is echoed by Paul Tournier and Billy Graham. Tournier says that his whole book *Learning to Grow Old* is for people of all ages, quoting the eminent psychologist Carl Jung when he says,

> It is a law of life that it must always move forward. 'Not to take this forward step,' writes Jung, is to fail 'to see that to refuse to grow old is as foolish as to refuse to leave behind one's childhood . . . It is impossible to live through the evening of life in accordance with the programmes appropriate to the morning, since what had great importance then will have very little now,

and the truth of the morning will be the error of the evening.'[5]

Life changes, sometimes gradually, sometimes more dramatically. Retirement is often the latter, and preparations are vital. We need to be ready and, as Graham urges, 'The best way to meet the challenges of old age is to prepare for them now, before they arrive.'[6] Whether we think about it or not, society at large see retirees as a completely different social group. If you do not believe this, wait until you retire and then, even a few weeks later, go back to your old workplace and see the reaction on the faces of those who were your colleagues. You are now yesterday's person; the work has moved on without you, and your return is an embarrassment, a reminder of times gone by. Yours is a new world to you, but an unknown one to these people who do not quite know what to say.

Life will change financially, which may have huge implications if you have not planned carefully. The media constantly remind us of how older people struggle as they try to juggle with much less money than they had when working. 'Health warning for elderly as higher energy bills bite', screams the headline. The article that is under these words uses the emotive word 'fear' as it says,

Two fifths of people in Britain aged sixty-five and over feared that the cold weather would lead to rising bills – and 11 per cent, equivalent to 1.3 million people, said that they could not afford the increase. Twelve per cent said that their health already suffered because they limited the amount of heating they used and 20 per cent ate less – or bought cheaper food to offset high energy costs. More than a third (thirty-eight per cent) rationed their energy because of the cost, according to a poll of 2,000 correspondents aged sixty-five and over by Comparethemarket, the comparison website.

Pensioners' decisions to limit their energy use comes despite 88 per cent believing that low temperatures present a serious health threat to older people. According to Age UK, each winter one older person dies from the cold every seven minutes.[7]

This alarming article appeared in *The Times* in January 2018, immediately under another one headed, 'A million lonely pensioners left to starve in their own homes'. Here are some extracts from the article:

As many as a million older people are starving in their homes through loneliness according to MPs who have called on ministers to redirect funds into schemes such as lunch clubs.

Isolation from relatives and friends is a bigger cause of malnutrition in the elderly than poverty, they say, and the winter fuel allowance should be means tested to free money for meals on wheels and lunch clubs. The all party parliamentary group on hunger . . . reports cases where people have gone without food for weeks after losing a partner or wasted away over many months because they have no one to help them cook. Others have gone hungry because they cannot get to the shops. Some have been banned from supermarkets for falling over.

The Times article quotes Frank Field, chairman of the parliamentary group, saying how 'there are malnourished older people in this country spending two or three months withering away in their own homes, with some entering hospital weighing five and a half stone with an infection, or following a fall, which keeps them there for several tortuous days, if not weeks.' The Prime Minister, the article quotes, said that loneliness was the 'sad reality of modern life' as she appointed Britain's first minister for loneliness the previous week.[8]

The key to all this is: getting ready. We should not be surprised that we are getting older, nor bury our heads in the sand and pretend it will never happen. These articles and books are saying the same thing: get your finances sorted out, get as many friends around you as you can, think through your money and your contacts, as well as maintaining your health as best you can. Further, to enable your family to avoid unseemly pressures, get a will written and decide where you would wish to live if and when you cannot look after yourself. This is known as a 'living will', so that if any incapacity arises, your family and friends will know what your wishes are. It is good to put in a name or names for who could act on your behalf, giving them a Power of Attorney. Saying 'it won't happen to me' is dangerously silly. Louise Morse calls one of her books *What's Age Got to Do with It?*[9] – the answer is, 'everything'.

The subtitle of Morse's book is *Living Out God's Purposes at All Ages*, which leads to what may be the most vital preparation of all: being ready for retirement spiritually. Are we ready for the great adventure of ageing with God's loving help? As Jim Packer says, 'Learning to live with one's old age is a spiritual discipline in itself.'[10] When Roger Hitchings lectures on retirement, he calls it 'The Gateway to New Opportunities'. His heading is echoed by Robert McCrum:

> I don't think ageing is the loss of youth. Ageing is ageing. Every stage of the life cycle is potentially interesting. And it's particularly interesting if you don't think elegiacally, if you don't think, 'What have I lost?' but instead, 'What can I do now?' There will be more possibilities when we are seventy.[11]

Are we ready for all the possibilities God has for us in our later years? Are we excited that there may well be time for the many things about which we have always been saying, 'I'll get around to it one day soon,' but that day never seemed to come? Now I have been retired some years, I am really glad that I sat down well before the day arrived and made a list of those things, because they are proving a blessing now. I found the stamp book my Gran gave me when I was eight and resolved to renew my love of stamp collecting. It is a slow process, but I now have a great collection which is still growing. I have rediscovered my old guitar, given to me in my teens. Our home group has no music leader, so the fingers have learned again how to get around the chords and we sing joyfully together. Now one of my grandchildren is toying with a ukulele, and my little banjulele has reappeared as well.

Old skills can resurface for the glory of God and our pleasure. We can have lovely new things to do from old things we once enjoyed. Daytime TV and games on the iPad and computer are very addictive but too often soul-destroying. On the other hand, other activities are important: keeping fit in body by walking for the morning paper rather than having it delivered, and keeping fit in mind by good reading and struggling with a tough crossword (in my retirement I won *The Times* crossword for the third time!) are very healthy exercises. The old adage, 'Use it or lose it' is true.

So – are you ready for the adventure of retirement? Then – let's do it.

What to do

My friend Norman Bussey recently died at the age of 94. He was my Bible Class leader when I was a teenager, when he worked as a painter and decorator. He had come to faith in 1952 and, despite the sorrow he and his wife, Margaret, felt at having no children, they cared for many youngsters like me with their open door and a fine fellowship in their home. Norman was later ordained and, after a fruitful ministry, he and Margaret had to move to a nursing home because of Margaret's health. She died there some years before Norman.

This dear man, in his late eighties, came to terms with living alone in his room at the home and determined to be God's man there. The receptionist told me how Norman would come down each morning and greet her with a warm smile. One day he noticed her sadness and was told that she had been diagnosed with breast cancer. There and then he offered to pray for her – an offer gladly accepted. Every day after that he came down, gave her a hug (very old folk can get away with that if not rebuffed!) and prayed. 'It meant the world to me,' she told me. 'The prayers from Norman helped me to overcome the stress and strains that come with cancer.'

Every Sunday – even at 94 – Norman held a little service for those in the home. He sent away for a CD of Moody and Sankey hymns, got the words printed, and prepared a talk for each week. Even more, Norman told me, 'There's never a day goes by but I talk with someone about Jesus.' The carers in the home were from many other countries, often lonely and so glad to hear of God's love. One of these told me, 'Norman loved his friends and family, he enjoyed his life and his Christianity. His door was always open.' I wonder if I will be sharing Jesus with others and leading services at 94? Back to 'use it or lose it': I intend with God's help to use it this year and then . . .

Speaking of which, another birthday happened yesterday, as I write (they seem to be coming round each year at present), and a card from an alleged friend had, within it, words from a former Warden of All Souls College, Oxford:

I'm accustomed to my deafness
To my dentures I'm resigned.
I can cope with my bifocals:
But – oh dear – I miss my mind![12]

Whether we can do as Norman did up to a few weeks before his death will depend on several factors, including our mental and physical capacities. As Lingiardi and McWilliams say,

> Research in ageing must begin with recognition that one of the most robust findings is heterogeneity: there is tremendous variability associated with ageing. Indeed, some older adults function well as heads of state, whilst others cannot recognize their own family members or even get out of bed.[13]

But one factor will predominate: will we, like Norman, look at our retirement from a Christian perspective? It is very possible to forget this key ingredient. In a book spanning 400 pages, Gratton and Scott's *The 100-Year Life* manages to leave God out of all their suggestions for how we can live in our later years:

> Qualitatively there are sure to be differences when lives elongate, as people make their own decisions about how to spend this extra time. The opportunities are vast: they could spend it working in order to build their financial assets; developing their skills; taking time out with friends, their partner and children; keeping healthy; going on sabbaticals; broadening their networks; or exploring different jobs and different ways of living.[14]

The nearest this tome gets to anything even remotely religious is in connection with whether we make things better for ourselves financially: 'In a long life, you have the potential to build a Cathedral rather than a shopping mall'![15] God gets left out very easily in a secular world. In a similar vein, the brilliantly written *A History of Modern Britain*,[16] by the political journalist and broadcaster Andrew Marr, gives a wonderful sweep of life from 1945 onwards, yet almost anything to do with Christianity during this period, in a book over 600 pages long, is not to be found. The several great Missions led by Billy Graham, the life and work of the Church, find no place in its pages. God is simply not relevant.

In this, we are little different from the United States, despite their greater church attendance. *The 100-Year Life* describes the situation there – notice how 'church' gets just one brief mention:

> One way of thinking about leisure and the allocation of time is to consider how much enjoyment people take from different activities, the results of a U.S. survey showed that top of the most enjoyable activities are sex, playing sport, fishing, art and music, socialising in bars and lounges, playing with the kids, talking and reading to kids, sleeping, going to church and going to the movies. At the bottom of the list are work, baby care, homework, second job, cooking and working at home, child care, commuting, errands, home repairs, laundry and dealing with children's health issues.[17]

There you are: a huge list to choose from in your later years. Retirement has a wealth of 'to do' opportunities. To even suggest that we should be doing things with and for God in the age in which we live may appear radical and countercultural. So – let's be radical. Let's fly in the face of our culture and see what we can do that is specifically and unashamedly for Jesus.

Doing retirement with God

In my previous research into the relationship between older people and the Church,[18] it was saddening to find that nearly 40 per cent of all those I interviewed felt there was nothing they could now do with or for the Church. Some said they were 'too long in the tooth', others that they 'did not fit in' and, perhaps most honestly, 'there's a lot I could do but, mea culpa, I share the common reluctance to get involved.'

The good news is that, in my research then and in meetings with many Christians for the purposes of this current book, many more are enthusiastic about their involvement. Their stories may help us see that there is much we can do. Of course, we will always take as a given that it depends on our strength of body and mind, as well as the spirit being willing. Tom and Judy are a husband and wife in their eighties, neither in good health. Despite wondering how much longer they can go on, they feel that, while they have a bit of energy, they can do 'a bit more'. In a very big living room in their home on the edge of a Midlands city, every Sunday evening finds them welcoming mainly older Christians to an informal service, there being no evening services in the surrounding area. Over tea and coffee, fellowship is enjoyed, with the service blessing and inspiring all who come. 'God has given us strength and a home that is for God: we praise the Lord for how he has blessed us.'

Sometimes Tom and Judy push the boat out, with over 70 coming to a Christmas carol service and an annual 'Prayer for Israel' gathering. They host two weekly Bible study groups. The key thing which comes through their testimony was how they themselves were blessed as they offered their home to God. Judy told me it is 'a joy to serve other people', while Tom loves being a 'people person'. At least half who come are single, having lost partners, so the friendship and fellowship relieve their loneliness. Not all of us have big homes, but having a few friends round for a time when we can worship and pray together should be possible for most of us.

One of the things we older ones need to lose is a false modesty. Our lifetime of experience is now of value. Sometimes through our mistakes, sometimes through the many things we have done well, we have much to offer as Christians. Elizabeth is also in her eighties. Her working life has been spent as an exceptionally brilliant doctor, specializing in paediatrics and child protection. She has learned over many years how to get alongside the vulnerable. At her age, should she 'sit and knit', 'go to tea parties' – or realize, in her words, that 'life is worth it if you make even a little difference'? Elizabeth has made the deliberate decision to take this latter course. She acts as a spiritual director to a church leader, leads a weekly meditation and a monthly prayer meeting.

It is all about attitude. 'I can't retire,' she told me. 'Life's exciting. I have a burning desire to be with people, to share and to learn. My brain is still active; how can I close it down?' Almost every day will find Elizabeth counselling someone on the phone, while she is still working on a church network concerned with non-violence to children. 'I'm not for giving up – I have a zest for life and an enormous zeal for God.' She is a great example of using our life skills for God's glory, both in her own home and in the wider community.

National surveys have shown for decades that, compared with the rest of the population, an increasing proportion of older people volunteer to help in religious activities.[19] In many a rural church, if the older ages did not take a lead, there would not be a church. Those of us who live in rural communities do not have the luxury of choice enjoyed by city folk. Where I live, we have one village store and one village church. These days, the lack of shops is overcome by supermarkets being willing to deliver most of our shopping needs (if we have access to the internet). But there is no mobile church. Our village has the Anglican church – the only choice – and the bus does not run early enough on Sunday mornings to get older car-less Christians to the nearest alternatives over five miles away. As a result, if our village is to have a place of worship, someone has to keep it going.

The vicar has four parish churches and lives in the vicarage in a neighbouring village, so he is not always on hand (or always there, as two long interregna in the last ten years have proved). In an ageing congregation of fewer than 20, four people do the bulk of the work. Margaret and Ian all but break their backs caring for the enormous church-yard, while Norma and Andrew look after all things inside the church. Andrew is our only churchwarden and spends inordinate amounts of time keeping the show on the road – from opening and closing the door each day, sorting out services and preparing the Communion table, to supervising funerals and arranging school visits. Both these married couples passed 70 several years ago and in another very few years, will not have the strength to carry on. The challenge is that there seems to be no one to replace them. In a village of 2,000 people, who would be horrified if the church were to close, this wonderful work by retirees is absolutely vital for local worship.

Andrew, the churchwarden, is not sure how he got so heavily into the work he does. 'It just sort of happened' he confessed. After a busy life as a medical doctor early on in Africa and then in English towns, he could have settled down quietly in the pew. He knows he has a serious role, representing the Bishop in our church. He would prefer if someone young were there to take over and has no answer as to who will be doing his job in ten years' time. He acknowledges he is not as strong as he would like, despite long walks each Monday. 'I'm a sort of Trustee until someone comes to take over. I'd hate to see our church with no one doing anything. But it needs a person who will do it from their heart.' So why does he do it? 'It's a sort of combination of my faith in Jesus, a family work ethic and listening to the epistle of James!' Of course there are others – Andrew says he is so grateful to his wife Norma for her support, patience and understanding. There are helpers who act as secretary, treasurer, Bible readers and so on. But we would be lost without him.

Packer has a telling remark: he says how church leaders 'behave as though spiritual gifts and ministry skills wither with age. But,' he goes on, 'they don't, what happens, rather, is that they atrophy with disuse.'[20] Merchant also puts it strongly: 'Perhaps it is that retirement is not a sacrament of the church, so it doesn't fall into the church calendar.'[21]

What seems to be needed is a new working partnership between churches and older people, whereby each benefits from the other. Packer makes this further observation:

> The assumption that was general in my youth that only a small minority would be fit and active after about seventy, has become a thing of the past. Churches, society and seniors themselves are still adjusting to the likelihood that most Christians who hit seventy still have before them at least a decade in which some form of adult service for Christ remains practicable.[22]

I would have to suggest that Packer may have erred on the side of caution with the word 'decade'. Even for the over eighties, a bit more of give and take on each side of the church and older members will afford blessings for both. Pam and John are still enthusiastic to be used by God in their eighties. They love to be involved, but need the church to have mercy on their struggles with a worship style that is so avant-garde as to be beyond them. They have had the courage and the sense to move from one church where the worship style seemed only to be centred on a student population from a nearby university, where they not only felt unneeded but where no effort was made to accommodate the local older parishioners. Now another local city church has opened its arms to them, and they feel they have a new lease on life.[23]

The new church is warm and welcoming, and they have quickly been accepted – and have accepted the ethos of the church. It is always give and take. The minister and his wife came to see them within a couple of weeks of their joining, and now they are involved. Pam and John told me a most interesting thing: because they now make a contribution, it keeps them closer as a couple and closer to God. Pam is restricted physically, but she can still share. 'I like to participate, rather than being "pew fodder",' was her delightful way of expressing how she felt. The church is open for activities every single day, and they love that. They are part of the prayer ministry, share in the mid-week services and help with the readings. 'We feel blessed and hope to be a blessing to others,' was how John summed it up. That is what I meant when I said that co-operation between church and older members is the secret. It is the way forward for both.

Reaching out

I want to look in the next two chapters at how we can come to faith in our later years, and how those of us who are Christians can reach out to others. But in the context of re-tirement, it is good to see how this co-operation can work in evangelism. There is a splendid opportunity for the church to harness the life experiences of their seniors in helping others come to faith.

John Piper's book *Desiring God* is now over 30 years old and, in a fast-changing world, is now a little dated. His chapter 'Missions: the Battle Cry of Christian Hedonism' begins with a rather startling quotation from Ralph Winter, founder of the United States Center for World Mission:

Most men don't die of old age, they die of retirement. I read somewhere that half of the men retiring in the state of New York die within two years. Save your life and you'll lose it. Just like other drugs, other psychological addictions, retirement is a virulent disease, not a blessing.[23]

The reason Piper quotes this is to say this about Winter's words:

Not only does he call retired Christians to quit throwing their lives away on the golf course when they could be giving themselves to the global cause of Christ, but he also calls students to go hard after the fullest and deepest joy of life.[24]

The point that struck me when I read this was the need for us older ones not to spend so much time playing golf, or whatever we do, that we fail to be part of Christ's 'global cause'. There is so much we can do with and for Jesus. Norman Critchell, one-time director of the now defunct Outlook Trust, speaks with enthusiasm about how churches can use their older members in outreach. Like me, he is a fan of 'Senior Alpha', the Alpha course re-written and shaped for those who are older, helping many to think through the call of Christ on their lives as they age. He told me, 'There are enthusiastic older people who want to reach out: they need resourcing and help with the 'how to".' He spoke of one church leader telling him of older people who only came into the church, sat and went home. 'I told him to encourage them. We can look at holidays at home, weekly meetings and showing our older members how they can reach out to others. Our older people can be a missionary force today, along with younger people. Older people have so much in them to give.'

I want to blow a trumpet for the diocese in which I live – the most northerly in England – Newcastle. We have our own task group that works on 'the gift of years'. Jackie Thompson, its chair, told me of its three strands. The first is evangelism, which has such diverse ideas as a Costa Coffee Club, a men's breakfast, a café church, a book club – and bizarrely, line dancing! How great to see them thinking outside the box in their aim to reach out to those who have little or no connection with the Church and seem far from God.

Strand two is called 'Reconnecting', which is a natural progression from evangelism. 'We know that there are many in the congregations with skills that are no longer being used – we want to encourage including people and using skills that they have, to give them a sense of involvement and usefulness.' These words from Jackie are heartening, and her task group has mapped out the Diocese to see how things might work. The plan includes ideas for churches: 'Time for a comeback', 'A prayer shawl ministry', 'A prayer chain', 'The gift of years Newcastle', and 'Come celebrate Christmas'. I love this – such a positive approach, with do-able titles and ideas.

The third strand is based on a concept from Australia, called 'Anna Chaplaincy', a new Spiritual Care course, which began in Newcastle in February 2018 and is the first in England. It is to help ministry in care homes and includes training, fundraising, Communion, games, tea and chat and a seniors 'Messy Vintage Church', with crafts, painting, singing and so on. Taking all these strands together, the potential for many to be involved both in giving and receiving is enormous. I love the proactive approach, the 'let's do it' style. It throws out a challenge to the rest of the country and other denominations to see what they can do.

In my helter-skelter enthusiasm, I need to pause here to offer an explanation. Any author writes from a personal viewpoint and within their own experience. I am no exception. The last few paragraphs underline my being an Anglican. I am, first and foremost, a Bible-believing Christian and have worked with and enjoyed fellowship with multitudes of Christians from all denominations. I have sought not to write from a limited vision, but I admit that quite a number of my examples come from areas with which I am more closely associated. I ask my readers to have mercy!

This is especially requested as I turn, briefly, to an area that I realize is controversial and that will ring alarm bells with some. I refer to what is called 'Messy Church'. A major part of the difficulty is its name because in many instances it is, at best, a pre-church bridge to the real thing rather than church itself. I have already looked in some depth at what the word 'church' means. Some will see 'Messy Church' as being simplistic children's stories and crafts – and they may be right, drawing the conclusion that this is not 'proper' church. But with so many in our present day being so far from God, I would defend the place of building the bridges and stepping stones that are essential to bring people into the Church. The key to understanding what now follows is this: it has mobilized many in their later lives in the service of the Church and the community. As an encourager of this, as well as my being an evangelist who wants to see people brought nearer to Jesus, however inadequate the means may seem, I offer the next few paragraphs.

For me, Messy Church at its best can be an exciting idea for reaching out to un-churched families, parents and children. How does this fit into a book like this? The answer is, it is predominately older people who are the powerhouse to make it happen. The plan of Messy Church is now well known, usually happening after school or at a time away from Sunday services, when parents and children get together in a church or school hall or other suitable meeting place, for fun, creative activities, some food and the sharing of the Christian message. I was invited to the one our churches locally put on each month one day after school in a village hall. It was a revelation.

Led by Helen Bishopp, a lively 60-something leader in our churches, the majority of those helping are over 70, with a few over 80. Some make the refreshments, some sit with the children and help with the crafts, one orders all the materials needed, all join in the prayer time at the beginning and all help to make the overtly spiritual input meaningful. I was there for their pre-Christmas meeting. There was a wealth of activities – making crowns, paper chains, Christmas wreaths and painting – and then a very good DVD from the Bible Societies.

Helen told me how she had felt challenged, as she was now retired herself, to do something for the children who came to the annual holiday club, run for a week in the summer holidays. The parents were saying they wished there was something during the rest of the year (like many churches, we have no Sunday school). The team that helped with the holiday club was already in place and, from its outset, Messy Church has been a big hit. Older people who simply came to church now have a wonderful role to play, each playing to their strengths and none being pushed too far. As Helen says, she is one of the younger leaders, with some 20 in all. She is realistic: these parents and children are unlikely to come to the older-style Sunday services at the moment, and the church must work hard to bridge the gap.

Tim Sanderson is the Assistant Minister at Holy Trinity Jesmond, Newcastle, and leads training for Messy Church. His is a city church that, unlike ours, has a membership where half are under 40 years old. But here is the remarkable thing: although their own Messy Church aims to involve younger leaders and helpers, 'We couldn't run it without our older people.' The majority he trains in the area are retired. 'The 65-plus are the engine of Messy Church,' he told me. The Founder and Team Leader for Messy Church nationally agrees with this. Lucy Moore says how 'older people are vital to Messy Church.' Significantly, she told me that they 'often find a new energy in their own discipleship through doing it'. Like the Newcastle Diocese, Messy Church has branched out into Messy Vintage. Lucy also said, 'We love the intergenerational aspect of Messy Church and the huge benefits that older people bring – it keeps on proving that openness to God and to new experiences is not restricted to a single generation but is there for everyone, and older people bring maturity of discipleship, the generosity of (great) grandparents, the skills younger generations may not yet have and, just by their presence, witness to the fact that God cares about us and we are 'useful' to him right up to the end of life: we all matter, young and old.'

Research done by Suzanne Morton, the Community Outreach Worker at Greenhill Methodist Church, backs up the fact that most of those who help with Messy Church are older and that many are receiving almost more than they give as they are involved. It is a brilliant way those in their later years can do something for God and for the blessing of upcoming generations.

Just in case you think I might have a bias towards the North (I do, but I try not to let it show), there is a church in the South that is doing an astonishing amount with and for its seniors, and for those in later years around them. Winchester Baptist Church has really pushed the boat out with its 'Mission to Seniors at Winchester Baptist Church'. It is committed to 'Developing and Maintaining a Strategy for Mission', all written down in their 'Vision to Reality' booklet. They not only have a Holiday at Home, but Elizabeth Stacey has written a 'How to run one'. Not only do they have a seniors' Christmas Nativity Celebration, but have a beautifully produced full-colour programme for it. They have their own presentation of a Pilgrim's Progress. They show how, with enthusiasm, there is much that can be done.[25]

Close to home

I may have kept the best and most important area of what can be done in retirement for the last section of this chapter. There is one special and unique way in which we older ones have a wonderfully privileged role to play: in our own families. If ever we want to 'do' old age well, this is it. Let me look at three specific areas. I do acknowledge, in what follows, that many people do not have children, lots of us still have our spouses, while others have either never married or live in different kinds of partnerships. We live in a world full of variety, and I trust I will be as comprehensive as I can in this current section.

First, what about our marriages? In conversation with Rob Merchant, he urged me to include the warning that we are seeing an alarming increase in divorces among the over-sixties. The problem, he says, and I agree with him, is that it is easy to spend so much time with our work and our children that we fail to invest in each other. We may not have given to each other in the way we have given to everyone else, and when it comes down to the two of us in retirement, things are in danger of falling apart. There is another danger: as we see the younger generation getting their divorces, perhaps even including our own children, we discover that this makes it possible to go down this same route.

As we invest in our future in our later lives, we need to re-invest in our marriages. When speaking to Christian leaders, I often challenge them as to when was the last time they said to their partner 'I love you'. Love is a flame that needs continual fanning. Ruth and I are learning this all the time. Every time I go away for more than a couple of days on a speaking mission, Ruth slips an 'I love you' card into my suitcase, while I leave one under her pillow. If I could show her my love – and speak of it – when we were courting, how much more I should do that each day after these many years of marriage.

Second, we need to 'do' our retirement with our children. I am always honoured when one or another of our four sons (we only do girls with our grandchildren!) calls us for some advice or help. 'Is not wisdom found among the aged? Does not long life bring understanding?' asks the book of Job (12.12). Whether we like it or not, our adult children are keenly aware of our own ageing and are, both consciously and unconsciously, watching us to see how we get it right – or, at least, avoid getting it wrong.

In the context of the people of Israel remembering their history, Psalm 78 has some challenging words for us, with verses 3 and 4 saying this:

What we have heard and known,
what our fathers have told us.
We will not hide them from our children;
we will tell the next generation
the praiseworthy deeds of the Lord,
his powers and the wonders he has done.

As God works in and through my life and my ministry in my later days, I want all my children to see that God still loves me and has plans in and for my life. Then they will know that they do not need to give up, because God will be with them and for them as well. I often use the first half of Psalm 71.18 when speaking to older people, as one of the most touching prayers we can pray. I have to remind myself that the second half of the verse is for me:

Even when I am old and grey
do not forsake me, O God,
till I declare your power to the next generation,
your might to all who are to come.

The way I see my sons and their wives, I am keenly aware of the many struggles they have, as well as their joys. I want to be there for them all, sons and daughters-in-law alike. The expression 'pump up their tyres' is key for me. Whoever knocks them, criticizes them and pushes them down, I want to be their encourager, enthusing for them and, above all, constantly praying for them.

This brings me to those amazing gifts in my life, my ten grandchildren – seven boys and three girls – of whom I am passionately fond. If ever a verse challenges me at the moment, it is where Paul speaks to his young protégé, Timothy, of how this young man came to faith:

I have been reminded of your sincere faith, which first lived in your grandmother Lois and in your mother Eunice and, I am persuaded, now lives in you also (2 Timothy 1.5).

The challenge for me is twofold: how wonderful to see the Christian faith passed down the generations and that a grandparent played her part, as I want to play a part in passing on the faith to my grandchildren. The other challenge is to see who is not mentioned: where are Dad and Grandpa? We don't know, but it prompts the thought that there are too many families where the men's faith is conspicuously absent; please, may, as the old chorus says, 'the beauty of Jesus be seen in me'.[26]

> A harmonious intimacy between grandparents and grandchildren can very often be an incomparably precious blessing for both. For a retired person there are few activities more wonderful than taking an interest in his grandchildren: going for a walk with one of them, teaching him to observe Nature and life; making a kite or an aeroplane with another, and trying it out; or else putting together a stamp collection. And what an event for the child – to be given such a personal welcome, to be taken aside, away from his brothers and sisters, and to be listened to and understood.[27]

These are great words of encouragement from old Dr Tournier, if a little old-fashioned. With a slight interpretation and updating, they make me want to do more with my grandchildren. I do stamps with one, watch football with another and admire the intricacies of ballet while watching one of my granddaughters – a pleasant change from standing by freezing rugby pitches when my lads were young!

As someone with a big invisible 'L' plate in this area – as I write, we await our first teenager – I am taking advice from all and sundry who have got further down the road. Clifford Pond is wise with this caution:

> We must be careful in interfering in family disputes, no matter whether adults or children are involved: they have to work the problems out for themselves. This means that you and I should keep quiet even when we are tempted very strongly to intervene.
>
> We may disapprove of the way our grandchildren are being trained or, we may think of their lack of training, and again we are tempted to intrude. As David Gay suggests, it is right for us to give advice if we are consulted, but apart from that it is all too easy to make things worse by being constantly critical, or even trying to take matters into our own hands. This requires a great deal of patience, and we must exercise self control as the Lord enables us.[28]

While I accept these caveats and seek to follow them, I do believe that both grandparents and great-grandparents have really important places and parts to play in the family. Ruth and I pray every day for these lovely children as they grow up in a world that seems increasingly alien to anyone who confesses loving Jesus. We are so glad for 'Facetime', so we can see them when we are not actually present. My oldest grandchild has his own mobile phone, and he and I exchange wacky texts. I believe very strongly in being an encourager; there are enough people out there to put these children down. I am determined to be a Grandpa who picks them up. You will have worked out that this being a Grandpa is one of my greatest joys. I want each and every one of my grandchildren to know that. I thank God for this huge blessing, and I try to pass on that blessing to them.

Looking back through this chapter, I am encouraged to see how much we older ones can do. May God give us the strength and the power of His Holy Spirit to get it right.

8

Can't teach an old dog?

There is a singer who delights in the unlikely name of 'Seasick Steve', one of whose songs bears the title of an old proverb: 'You can't teach an old dog new tricks.'[1] In it, he bemoans his plight, says he has been the way he is for a long, long time and wishes he could put a little fire in his life. The question is whether he – and the proverb – are right. Are we ever too late to change?

When I was a lad, growing up in Harrogate, Yorkshire, in the 50s, an old man lived a couple of roads away from our house, by the name of Richard Hudson Pope. He was a children's evangelist, and he had done no less than 51 years of beach missions consecutively each summer, bettered only by his wife, who had clocked up 52. On one of these missions, a boy had approached him with the question, 'Mr Pope, am I too young to come to Jesus?' The following morning, Hudson Pope taught the children, including the boy, a chorus he had written overnight:

I'm not too young to come to Jesus,
For He loves a little child;
And I need Him, and He needs me,
And, O! How happy we shall be
If I come now.[2]

I remember this lifelong evangelist singing this at our piano, which he always attacked with vigour, not long before he died in his eighties. His eyes sparkled as his fingers battered out the notes, his old voice full of joy. His experience had been that young children could know Jesus personally. Alas, some of us go through our entire lives without this experience so – now – we fear it is too late for us. Would it be possible to rewrite Hudson Pope's words to say 'I'm not too old to come to Jesus?' There is great news: you are not too old. Let me prove that to you.

Starting over

'You are old, Father William', the young man said
'And your hair has become very white;
And yet you incessantly stand on your head –
Do you think, at your age, it is right?'

'In my youth', Father William replied to his son,
'I feared it might injure the brain;
But now that I'm perfectly sure I have none,
Why, I do it again and again.'[3]

This splendid opening to Alice's 'Advice from a Caterpillar' would be atypical of how many see us in our older years – people who deserve a little humour, as they start to patronize us, we sad old people who cannot now change. Lewis Carroll is suggesting here that the ageing process has now taken Father William backwards rather than forwards and he cannot now improve. We are the old dogs who cannot be taught new things. There is really no hope for us. If we are not careful, we ourselves begin to believe it is true. Our minds and hearts are like our bodies, unable to do what we once could, we think. My mother-in-law's arthritic hands mean that she cannot get round the intricacies of a complicated scherzo on her piano. There is no such thing as a 'new lamp for old' from Aladdin's cave.[4] Of course it is too late to change.

Stay with me here. This is no time for calling it a day. We, like the others, have left out a key factor. I have a friend called Chris, who told me the story of her dad. His name was Tom, described by his daughter as unconventional, frustrating, funny, wasteful – and stubborn. Chris and her sister Anne were (and are) committed Christians, but whenever a question of 'faith' arose, Tom's perennial answer was 'I'm not interested. End of story.' It was all rather frustrating for a family where all but Tom had, in different ways, come to know and follow Jesus. They detected that Tom's wartime experiences, the sudden loss of his mother at quite a young age and a strained relationship with his own father were factors that caused this, making anything to do with God a no-go area.

Things started to change when Tom had to nurse his ailing wife over a period of 20 years, bringing out a kinder and more caring side to his character, not seen before. After her death (we are in 2007 by now), Tom suffered minor strokes, and it became clear he was suffering from vascular dementia. He had to move from his own bungalow to another town where Anne lived and then into a friendly care home where he could be looked after. He got on well there, and one day saw a programme on the television about the Salvation Army. In his confusion Tom told his daughter that he thought he was a member of the Salvation Army, which was definitely odd, to say the least.

As we will see in Chapter 12, it is not helpful to contradict a dementia sufferer, so Anne went along with his 'membership' and took him to the monthly Songs of Praise at the Salvation Army in the town. Well done, Army, for the warm welcome and for treating Tom with respect and affection, which started something special. Tom loved the monthly services and looked forward to them. His changed state of mind made him forget he had been angry with God and that he did not want to have anything to do with faith. His carefully assembled barriers were gone. Dementia sufferers, as we will see, often have recent forgetfulness, but long-ago memories may become fresh again.

So it was that Tom told his far-off story. When he was a young child on the streets of London, with nowhere to go in bad weather, the Salvation Army would let him sit in the dry part of the bandstand with them. He also remembered when, as a vulnerable young sailor in New York, it had again been the Salvation Army who had helped him and given him money. Long forgotten acts of kindness shown many years before were now recalled with gratitude. Chris and Anne told me how especially clear it was that the lovely Christian music was reaching deep into Tom's understanding and, over time, he would love to sing and join in with enthusiasm. This was sometimes a little tricky, as he would sit near the front and conduct the band – very badly – so they had to try hard not to look at him!

Although Tom could not talk very logically about faith, he had clearly discovered that he had a Heavenly Father who loved him. Grace before meals became protracted times of prayer. At family weddings, when the hymns were sung, it was Tom who raised his hands in praise and worship. When the Anglican Church led a Communion service at the care home, he received the bread and wine for the first time. At a service at the Salvation Army in 2015, Tom sang with great feeling, 'When the roll is called up yonder, I'll be there.' Back at home, they brought him his bedtime drink, but it was not needed: he had slipped away to be with the Heavenly Father who had found him and embraced him those few years before.

What a remarkable story! And it relates back to another old man who also had a life-changing experience when he met Jesus many years before that. The man I refer to was called Nicodemus, who made a big mistake. He tried to sweet-talk Jesus, who has no need of being buttered up. Nicodemus was one of the top people in his day, a key teacher with years of experience and great learning. With his reputation at stake, he decided to meet Jesus at night, one to one, to find the truth about this person who was bringing in a new style of living. He tried to break the ice with a little flattery, addressing Jesus with a learned teacher's title:

Rabbi, we know you are a teacher who has come from God. For no one could perform the miraculous signs you are doing if God were not with him.

Alas, these words were not necessarily true. The Gospels show clearly that the religious leaders did not, in fact, believe

Jesus was from God, or that God was with him. It is possible that Nicodemus might have believed personally what he was saying, but his words did not fool Jesus. The whole encounter is in the first 16 verses of the Gospel of John, Chapter Three, in the Bible. I'm going to précis what happened.

Following this opening gambit by Nicodemus, Jesus immediately made a dramatic move, telling his visitor that, to see the kingdom of God, a person needed to be 'born again'. This expression has been used far too frequently in recent days, and this causes confusion as to its meaning; when Jesus used it, he meant that Nicodemus needed a brand new start with God. This intelligent man did not seem to understand. What Jesus was saying was in some ways revolutionary, yet in other ways echoed the familiar. Perhaps Nicodemus did grasp it there and then, or perhaps his understanding evolved to full belief later. When the other religious leaders argued sometime later for Jesus to be condemned, Nicodemus spoke up in his defence – and was criticized for it (John 7.50–52). He nailed his colours to the mast well and truly when he went, with great courage, to ask for the crucified and dead body of Jesus, to give him a decent burial in the tomb of Joseph of Arimathea (John 19.38–42), clearly showing his commitment to Jesus by then.

But this first night's meeting with Jesus finds Nicodemus asking with some astonishment how someone like him could be 'born again when he is old?' He joked that he could not go back to his mother's womb! No, no, replied Jesus; it means letting God's Spirit blow into your life, just like the wind blows. You cannot direct the wind, and you can't command God's Spirit.

Jesus understood the problems Nicodemus was having in following his argument, and he used two examples from the Scriptures (what we now call the Old Testament) to shed light on what he was saying. The first referred back to Ezekiel 36.25–26. Jesus tells Nicodemus that a person needs to be born of water and the Spirit (John 3.5). This would immediately ring bells with Nicodemus, as the words in Ezekiel say this:

> I will sprinkle clean water on you, and you will be clean. . . . I will give you a new heart and a new spirit in you; I will remove from you your heart of stone and given you a heart of flesh.'

Ezekiel proclaims that it is God who gives the new heart, so if we think we are too old to be born again, we are in danger of denying the power of God himself!

Then Jesus reminded Nicodemus of an old faraway story from the history of Israel, which would immediately be remembered by Nicodemus. One day, when Moses was leading the people of Israel back to their land and away from slavery, the people were bitten by snakes. To rescue them, God told Moses to put a brass snake on a pole so that, to prove they were trusting God, if they looked at the pole it was their way of showing their trust and then they were healed.

Nicodemus would have understood that, but would have been shocked to hear what Jesus then said:

> Just as Moses lifted up the snake in the desert, so the Son of Man must be lifted up, that everyone who

believes in him may have eternal life. For God so loved the world that he gave his one and only Son, that whoever believes in him shall not perish but have eternal life (John 3:15–16).

Here is the greatest news ever. We are like those people long ago: we have turned away from God. Now God has sent Jesus to be lifted up, not on a pole but on the cross, where he died for our sins. God raised him back to life, and he offers a new start, the chance to be 'born again' and receive 'eternal life'. For the purposes of this book, it is key to all that is being said to see that Nicodemus himself admitted he was 'old'. We who are older can come to Jesus to receive his forgiveness and new life, as his Holy Spirit comes to live in our hearts. I know this can happen, as I hear stories like that of Tom. Let me share another.

Because of a number of serious bereavements in my own life, I was encouraged to write a book entitled *Bereaved*, which contained this story told to me by my good friend Peter.[5] Joan was in her early seventies and, according to her son Peter, she was 'wearing out'. Sadly, the relationship between the two of them was not good. Brought up in Ceylon (now Sri Lanka), where Joan's husband was a tea planter, Peter saw his mother for a couple of hours a day by appointment: those were the days of colonialism and nannies! Time away at boarding school, and then his parents' divorce and Joan's remarriage, further estranged them. When Peter returned to England with his wife, Jennifer, his mother, who had in the meantime moved to New Zealand and was now a widow, fell ill.

This adversity led to a fresh beginning, Joan moving to England, near to Peter and Jennifer. Slowly, the old barriers came down, partly because of Peter's Christian commitment and the friendship shown by church friends to this older lady who knew no one. Joan's estrangement from her son faded away, as did her distance from God. At the age of 74, she attended a service in her local church. When an invitation was given for people to entrust their lives to the Lord Jesus Christ, Joan went forward to the front of the church to acknowledge publicly her new faith. Peter's joy was boundless. As Joan weakened physically, so she grew closer to Peter and Jennifer, and to the Lord she now loved.

Death approached, and Joan could not communicate or eat properly in her hospital bed. Peter would sit with her, relieved that she had a living and eternal faith, but often he was in tears at his mother's condition. A couple of days before Joan died, a friend was sitting with her. He started to read out loud from Psalm 23: 'The Lord is my shepherd.' Before he could continue, this dying, speechless lady said, quietly and distinctly, 'I shall not want.' They were the last words she ever spoke. What a splendid way to make your last farewell to life on earth!

I met up with Adrian Reynolds, one of the national leaders of the F.I.E.C. (the Fellowship of Independent Evangelical Churches), who told me of his friend Frank, to encourage others that we can have this life-changing experience of trusting ourselves to Jesus Christ even at the last minute. Frank was a tough cookie, an ex-soldier whose credo was 'I've been christened, so I'm fine,' to which Adrian had responded, 'If that's your argument on the Day of Judgement, you'll be found wanting.' Frank would not listen. Some while later he had a serious heart attack, landing him in hospital, and it was obvious he was not recovering: he could not speak, but he could hear.

Adrian decided he had to help Frank. He held his hand, and it was clear from Frank's bright eyes that he knew Adrian. 'If you know what I'm saying, squeeze my hand,' Adrian asked, receiving a squeeze. 'Frank – you've been rejecting the good news of Jesus, but you need to respond now. Are you listening?' There was a squeeze. 'Do you understand?' A squeeze. Adrian explained again to his old, dying friend the love of Jesus and how Frank could say 'yes'. He asked Frank to pray in his heart a prayer in which he could respond positively. At the end of the prayer, he asked Frank if he had prayed – and got a final squeeze of the hand. Adrian explained that this gave Frank an eternal life with God, whereupon Frank died. He was just in time.

I have to insert a word of caution here. When I go to Africa, I have to get used to what is known as 'Africa time'. This means that if a meeting is due to start at, say, 10, it actually gets going sometime after 11. Everyone finds this quite normal, and folk are amused that I should question this. It works, somehow, but occasionally causes a disaster. A bishop told me how he had turned up at Kilimanjaro airport 'Africa time', only to find his plane to the UK had left according to the clock. My father was a lawyer and a lay preacher. One day, a friend left a quotation on his desk for him to use in his preaching, from an anonymous source: 'Those who wait to repent at the eleventh hour often die at ten thirty.' God's word speaks only of 'today': 'Now is the time of God's favour, now is the day of salvation' (2 Corinthians 6.2).

The need

The Bible is brilliant! When I was young, there was so much in it just for me. In my middle years, I found such help and guidance. Now I'm a 'senior', I am finding that great chunks of the Scriptures are addressed to me in these later years. One such section is the little book hidden away at the back of the Old Testament, the prophecy of Joel. 'Hear this, you elders,' right at the beginning (1.2), means I had better read carefully. 'The word of the Lord' (1.1) gets right into the action straightaway, with a cold bath of unpleasant truth. Check this out, says God: when life goes wrong it is like an invasion of locusts. In West Africa I have seen what this means, where the little blighters eat every bit of green and devastate the entire countryside. God says that our lives are like that, eaten away by all the things that destroy us.

It is, sadly, true. I look back over my life with serious regrets. If only I hadn't said that unkind word. If only I'd helped that person. If my thoughts had been cleaner, purer, more generous, I would have been a better person. If only . . . I am good at bluffing and kidding myself, but the grim reality is that I have often broken God's law and fallen short of God's glory. 'Listen you elders' is a call to me. But God never tells us the bad news without coming straight to the good news. Joel is a brilliant book. Having told me that it has all gone wrong, he assures me that there is a way back from all my mistakes, my 'sins', to use an uncomfortable but honest word. Look at this:

Return to the Lord your God, for he is gracious and compassionate, slow to anger and abounding in love . . .

148

bring together the elders, gather the children . . . I will repay you for the years the locust has eaten . . . you will have plenty to eat, until you are full, and you will praise the name of the Lord your God, who has worked wonders for you.' (Joel 2.13,16; 3.25–26).

God makes a way back for us and, anticipating the death and resurrection of Jesus, after which God sent his Holy Spirit on the first Christians, goes on to say:

And afterwards, I will pour out my Spirit on all people. Your sons and daughters will prophecy, your old men will dream dreams, your young men will see visions, even on my servants, both men and women, I will pour out my Spirit in those days . . . and everyone who calls on the name of the Lord will be saved. (Joel 2.28,29,32).

Seeing the 'old men' in there, the 'men and women': I must urgently embrace what's on offer! I must embrace it now. As Jim Packer says:

I would only stress the urgency of entering, here and now, by faith, into a personal relation of discipleship to Christ, the invisibly present Saviour and Lord, as in and through the gospel he himself invites everyone to do. This will banish all fears about our future.[6]

A friend's story

Some years ago, when I lived in a cathedral city in the midlands of England, three doors up from our house lived an older couple called Pam and Basil. They had married late in life and were a delight to know. There came a time when Basil's health deteriorated, and he was unable to continue his commitment to the many committees on which he sat at the cathedral. He had been an architect and was hugely busy as a leader in this great church in his retirement. He was certainly one of the leading church-men of our city.

It was no surprise that he ended up being hospitalized, and we got almost daily bulletins from Pam of his continuing deterioration. I was very sad, as it seemed I was losing a good friend whose sharp wit was a foil to mine. He was always cynical, although not unkindly, of my 'style' of Christianity; he preferring the path of uncertainty to heart faith, ritual compared with a slightly more relaxed style. We sparred and happily accepted that the one would not convince the other.

The day came when Pam said that Basil had taken a serious turn for the worse, and I felt a great conviction that I should visit him in his hospital ward. As I left the house, I heard a quiet inner voice urging me to pop my little red Gideon New Testament in my pocket. The ward was quiet, and Basil was alone, propped up on pillows. It was no time for small talk nor our old banter. 'I'm dying,' he told me, and there was no arguing about this. I held his hand and never let go until I left. I got straight to the point, quietly, as we faced each other.

'Basil,' I asked, 'are you ready for this?'

'No,' he replied, and the tears started down his face. 'I don't know if I'm going to heaven.' This was a different Basil, the old bravado gone.

'This morning I was reading something wonderful in my Bible,' I told him. 'May I read it to you now?'

'Please.'

So I began: 'Do not let your hearts . . .' I was reading the first words of the Gospel of John, Chapter 14. It is a short passage used at many a funeral. I had only got these first words out when Basil started to say them with me. He was quoting by heart from the old Authorised Version, but it was almost the same as the one I was reading, so I read and he spoke in unison with me. Here is what we said together:

'Do not let your hearts be troubled. Trust in God; trust also in me. In my Father's house are many rooms; if it were not so, I would have told you. I am going there to prepare a place for you. And if I go and prepare a place for you, I will come back and take you to be with me, that you also may be with me where I am. You know the way to the place where I am going.'

Thomas said to him, 'Lord, we don't know where you are going, so how can we know the way?'

Jesus answered, 'I am the way and the truth and the life. No one comes to the Father except through me.' (John 14.1–6)

From anyone, let alone a man who is ill and near death, it is pretty impressive to hear such a long passage quoted by heart. I said as much to Basil.

'You know the words – but do you know them to be true in your heart?'
He began to weep again: 'No, I don't. But I want to.'

Very quietly and simply I explained how we need more than just churchgoing; we need a personal relationship with Jesus, we need to be forgiven our many sins and receive the risen Jesus in our hearts by his Holy Spirit. There was no sparring now. Basil nodded as I shared each of these thoughts with him.

'Basil, I'm not pushing you. Tell me what you want to do.'
'I want you to help me to be sure.'

So there, holding hands in the ward, I narrated the words of a little prayer I always use when I preach about God's good news:

Lord Jesus Christ,
I give you my whole life now.
Please live in my heart.
Wash away all my sins.
Fill me with your Holy Spirit.
Thank you that you will never leave me.

'Is that what you want?' I asked.
'Yes – it really is.'
'Then pray with me and mean it with all your
    heart.'

And we did, phrase by phrase. A peace came upon this dear man's face, and I prayed a 'thank you' and claimed the promise of Jesus that anyone who came to him, he would not turn them away (John 6.37). I left a man who had found the answer, as Jesus had come to him that morning. I never saw him again, because less than a fortnight later, I stood with hundreds of others in our cathedral as the full choir, cathedral clergy and two bishops preceded Basil's coffin. And I knew, in my sorrow, the certain joy that, for Basil, all was well.

It's for you!

The American evangelist Billy Graham has said this: 'It is never too late to begin building your life on the foundation of Jesus Christ and his will for your life.'[7] He is right. This personal relationship with the living and eternal God is for us older ones. Let me show that we can know this for ourselves from an intimate incident in the life of Jesus. I am telling the true story of a man who had been ill for many years; it is to be found in the first 15 verses of John Chapter Five. In those days, medicine was not too brilliant, to say the least. People went to all sorts of places for help including, in Jerusalem, a pool called Bethesda. It was surrounded by five covered colonnades, and the belief, possibly misguided, was that the waters of the pool would sometimes be disturbed, caused by an angel stirring them. Whoever got into the water first after this movement would be healed, the people thought.

As you would expect, great numbers came there with their disabilities – the blind, the lame, the paralysed. An older man had been an invalid for no less than 38 years, which is a very long time to be ill. Now, here is the thing that makes the account mean so much to me. Jesus came along, not to heal the whole crowd, but to meet this one man. I am constantly overwhelmed by Jesus' style of reaching out to each one of us as if we were the only person around. It actually says 'Jesus saw him lying there.' Just him. That is how he sees you and me. He was told that the man had had this condition for so long. In the same way, he knows how it is within us – just me, just you.

More than that, Jesus knew that this man had been looking for the answer to his need in the wrong place. The water was of no use. Even if the belief in its healing properties were true, the man never could get there first, lying on his mat. How hard we try to look for the right way for our lives – doing good, praying, churchgoing: even, as we used to say facetiously in our family when I was growing up, 'being kind to Granny and the cat'! Yet, it never really worked. It was Jesus this man needed, and it is Jesus we need.

After all, who else can forgive sins? No one else has died on the cross except him. No one else has been raised from the dead to live forevermore other than him. No one else and nothing else can give us the power to live other than his Holy Spirit. No one else can make heaven a reality for us other than the one who actually lives there – the same Lord

Jesus Christ. If we don't know that, it is great that Jesus does, which is why he asked the man if he wanted to be healed. Even then, the man could only protest that he had no one to put him into the pool, so stuck was he in his lostness. This was his problem, but it was not going to stop Jesus. Here is a direct quotation from John 5:8 and 9:

> Then Jesus said to him, 'Get up! Pick up your mat and walk'. At once the man was cured; he picked up his mat and walked.

The story goes on to show that Jesus had healed this man on the Jewish Sabbath, when work was prohibited, and this pitted him against the authorities. It merely underlines this fact: whatever the day, it was the right day for the disabled man. As I quoted earlier, 'Now is the day of salvation' (2 Corinthians 6.2). This response at the present time is further underlined by the writer to the Hebrews, quoting Psalm 95.7–8, 'Today, if you hear his voice, do not harden your hearts' (Hebrews 3.7). We need to answer God's call to our lives when it is made.

This wonderful encounter can be mirrored in each of our lives, as Jesus meets us. We may be old, but his call is there. I recall a delightful moment in my own ministry some years ago in Dundonald, Northern Ireland. We had had a week of mission in a very long church and had come to the final service. At the end, having shared the good news of the new life Jesus offers, I invited those in the congregation who wished to give their 'yes' to the Saviour to come forward to the front during the closing hymn, to show publicly that they were going to live a new life. In the first verse, at the very back, a very old couple looked at each other; I could see them as I watched the congregation. He was very tall, very erect, obviously an ex-military man. His wife was tiny beside him. They gave each other a little nod, stepped into the aisle and walked purposefully forward, hand in hand. It proved a challenge and inspiration to many others, and there was much rejoicing. We ran out of counsellors to talk to those who came.

The next morning we had a de-briefing. The lady who had been in charge of counselling was none other than the great missionary Helen Roseveare, who then made a singular confession. As a famous speaker herself, now retired, it had been many years since she had sat down and counselled one to one, being always the up-front speaker. Because they had run out of counsellors, she had had to get involved herself, and found the diminutive wife who had come first with her tall husband. To her own embarrassment and to general merriment, in this debriefing meeting, Helen said that, in her rather aggressive style she had had a conversation that went like this:

Helen: 'Why have you come forward?'
Lady: 'To give my life to Christ.'
Helen: 'Have you never done that before?'
Lady: 'No'
Helen: 'Why ever not?!'
Lady: 'I don't know and I feel like having a jolly good cry.'
Helen: 'Well then, let's have a jolly good cry together!'

Phew! Helen redeemed herself in the end, and an old lady was welcomed into the kingdom of God. It was so lovely that someone in her later life, along with her husband, could still respond to God's call and inspire others to do the same.

It is possible to go the other way. The secular writer Robert McCrum, whose book *Every Third Thought* is about facing up to dying, says something that, to me, is tragically poignant as he fails to take the necessary step of faith:

> Twenty something years ago, on my return from hospital, I found myself reading the King James Bible for the music of its language and the thrilling arrests of its narrative. Here was a cathedral of words whose expression of faith had no meaning for me, but whose sonorous periods can make you weep. I cherish the memory of that response.[8]

How sad for McCrum to be so near and yet so far, and what a contrast with the following story, told to me by my friend Winifred. George had dementia for about five years, and in the last couple of months had been going rapidly downhill. There had been no interaction with his two daughters for over a year, and they had a deep concern that he was slipping away and that they would not see him in eternity because he had not trusted Jesus for his salvation. As the two daughters sat either side of him in his bed, holding his hands, they grasped the nettle. They told their dad of their heartache, hoping he was listening.

'Dad,' one of them said. 'If you believe now in Jesus, that he died for you on the cross to be able to forgive all you have done in the past that was wrong, then nod your head.' Both daughters testify that he definitely nodded his head in agreement; they could hardly believe their eyes that he would make this positive response. Within a few hours, George died. When they found him, the usual jaw-dropping was absent. Instead his eyes were open, and there was a smile on his dead face. As Winifred, a doctor herself, told me, it seemed like a miracle of God's grace.

It is time for a 'miracle of God's grace' to be yours, too.

9

Share it!

The story is told of the great missionary C.T. Studd who, before he became a Christian, was a very rich man and a famous cricketer, playing for England. After he was converted, he approached a Christian leader to ask about some of the things he did in his life, about which he was now posing questions of himself as to whether they were right. He had a long list, including drinking alcohol, smoking, dancing, gambling – the list went on and on. The wise leader realized that Studd did not need a list of dos and don'ts in his new life, so gave some very sensible advice. He suggested that gambling was a bad idea, being a waste of money. Apart from that, his words were simple: 'Lead one person to Christ, and everything else will fall into place.'

Discerning readers of this book will have come to an obvious conclusion: your writer is an evangelist. It is my experience, over many years, that getting on with the positives tends to eliminate the negatives. As Bing Crosby and the Andrews Sisters used to sing, 'Accentuate the Positive'.[1] The more we do things with and for Jesus, the easier our choices become. There are many books on faith-sharing; if you go online, you will even find one called *Fifty Ways to Share Your Faith* by this author.[2] Much help can be found on how to do this with young people, but there is little on the subject of those in their later years. How can we get it right when reaching out to this great group of people who live all around us and who, in many cases, do not yet have a personal relationship with the Lord Jesus Christ? Rob Merchant concludes his entire book *Pioneering the Third Age* with these words:

> Finally, preach the gospel in season and out of season to men and women of all ages. Never exclude the older person from hearing the gospel of Jesus Christ from lack of awareness, preparation or desire. For Christ died for all.[3]

Merchant is right, both in his urging us to share our faith and in pointing out that some work needs to be done to get it right. Jim Packer takes this further, saying that we who are older have a special role here, comparing our present time with that of the early Church:

> The Roman Empire was a world that, like our world today, lacked any energising hope of its own, which explains why so many listened hungrily to the Christian message. And I go on to urge that recovering and reappropriating this hope is a prime task for us who are ageing today.[4]

With these encouragements, we need to look at the unique features of faith-sharing with the older generation, so we can go about it in the best possible way, making sure we do everything to help and nothing to hinder people hearing the call of Jesus Christ on their lives.

Problems

Before we come to look at some of the difficulties and challenges we may face, there is one which is within the Church and, perhaps, in our own subconsciousness. Rhena Taylor expresses it well:

> To seek to take the gospel of Christ to older people can be an unattractive mission field in our ageist society. There is little glamour attached (you won't easily grab the headlines in the Christian press) and possibly little recognition by your church. So check it out. Is this truly God's call to you?[5]

The question has already been raised: if we were to see considerable numbers of older people becoming Christians, would our churches be thrilled to see a great influx of this generation joining their already ageing congregations, compared with large numbers of young folk? Or would we see these newcomers as an unwelcome burden and drag on the life of the church? One would hope that this dreadful attitude would not be there. There are enough challenges without the Christian community putting up its own barriers. It would be good to assume a welcome for each and every newcomer, whoever they were.

I would want to take this even further: it is my continuing experience that there are considerable numbers, within our churches, of older people who do not have a deep certain faith in Jesus Christ. Our older generations may be the last groups who have simply 'gone to church'. They have been brought, or taken, to church or Sunday school as children and have just continued to go. Some have this as a lifetime habit, others have gone more intermittently, while some have returned in their later days. They do have a desire to worship, with a willingness by many to help out with the work within the church. I am finding, time and again, that many of these faithful churchgoers do want to make a real move in their lives, with a longing to come into a deep relationship with God through a personal trust in Jesus. In other words, I am not only going to look at helping those *outside* the church with our faith-sharing, but also at those who sit near us Sunday by Sunday and, yet deep inside, lack a real assurance of salvation.

This, in itself, can be a real problem. It is hard to acknowledge that our style of Christianity was not the correct one. All our 'doing good', the 'I do my best', 'I never did anybody any harm' has been a lifestyle, a credo, even a religious prop. To own up to a life that has been full of sin is anathema, particularly for those who have never done anything interestingly wrong. When I worked as a lawyer, my clients often got up to fascinatingly wrong activities. Most people I meet in church are seriously boring sinners. My own life is full of 'un' sins: I am un-friendly, un-kind, un-generous. For an older person to admit that life, thus far, has not been as God wants, is a tough call.

My father was a fairly straight preacher. He had the temerity to say, from the pulpit, that our good works, without a changed heart from Jesus, were worth nothing. He once had a man approach him at the end of a service, incandescent with rage, demanding, 'Are you telling me that I've been a churchwarden for 35 years and it doesn't mean anything?!' My father assured him that it was fine to do this good work, but the man needed a real heart-change, true forgiveness and a new life through the Holy Spirit. This message is outrageous if you are relying on your own good works for your salvation, but that reliance needs to be challenged in a loving way, for 'There is no one righteous, not even one' (Romans 3.10).

Coupled with this is the challenge of changing in any major way as one gets older. I regret that I was born too late to have been young during the computer revolution. There are so many gadgets, so many different and new ways of communicating, styles of social interacting that are so easy for my children and grandchildren but so hard to work out for me, who has not been born into this new era, but has come to it so late on. Change is almost impossible. Translate this into the spiritual realm. To move from one way of living to a completely new one in later life is asking a great deal. We get into a routine, a set pattern of living our lives, which makes a quantum leap of faith a really big deal. If you are a lifetime churchgoer, to move from a life of not having a deep, personal relationship with Jesus to one of knowing him as Lord and Saviour is a major step. If you are outside the church community, it can be even harder, because it will not only mean a new life, but becoming part of a new community, the community of faith. The church very rarely visited, mainly these days for funerals, will be a new experience, which may seem scary.

Pitfalls

There are two or three pitfalls to avoid as we try to help older people meet Jesus. The first is, if you are younger yourself, trying to suggest that you understand what it is like to be older. I had something happen in my life when I was only 22 that turned out to be an unexpected blessing: my mother died, very suddenly and unexpectedly. Before that, I remember going to a funeral and wondering what all the sorrow and tears were about. Surely the person who had died was now safely with Jesus, so we should be rejoicing? But no one seemed to be. It was all gloom and doom. Then mum died, and I knew. Yes, she was with Jesus, but that beautiful lady would never be with us until we got there as well. Even now, every Mothering Sunday I wish I could give her flowers. The best thing is to listen and learn, realizing we cannot enter the older person's world until we get there ourselves.

A second pitfall is one that is especially there with those we meet who are really old: beware of underestimating the intelligence of an older person. They almost certainly know more than you do. A little probing will lead to your finding what amazing lives they have led, what remarkable adventures they have been through and how special has been their line of work. Older people do not want to be addressed as if they were three years old, as if senility equated to infancy. 'Hello dear, how are you?' said in a soppy voice does not go down well. Treat an older person with respect and expect them to be able to understand every word you are saying – and to be able to see through your hypocrisy.

Which means, avoid the pitfall of patronizing, speaking down to a person with whom we want to share God's good news. The hint of 'I know better than you, more than you' will be an instant turn-off. Not patronizing includes respect, for example, being permitted by an older person to call them by their first name. In Tanzania's Swahili, an older person is always addressed, on any encounter, by a word of respect, which is then acknowledged by the older person. The two words have no translation into English, and the respect is rarely found in our culture either.

Enough of caveats! Let's be positive.

Potential

I love to preach on the first few verses of Luke 15. Jesus is accused of welcoming sinners – which is a great thing in itself. As a result, he tells the story of the shepherd who goes out to find the one lost sheep and brings it home with joy. He makes it clear that it is a picture of himself, bringing us home to God. It is my experience that, when I share this with older people, it is received with great openness and happiness. Many have tried for so long to reach out to God; what a relief to realize, finally, that Jesus is already seeking us. He said of himself, 'The Son of Man came to seek and to save what was lost' (Luke 19.10). In his meeting with Nicodemus, Jesus spoke of how the Holy Spirit blows into our lives like the wind: it is his doing, not ours (John 3.8). As we feel able to do less in our lives, it is a word of such encouragement that God sees our potential and comes to us with his love and his willingness to make us new.

The statistics quoted in earlier chapters reveal an enormous number of people who are older, giving a wonderful potential for those who could be followers of Jesus. Not only is this nothing to be afraid of, it could give a great body of Christians who, with the power of the Holy

Spirit and the wisdom of age, would bring new life to a needy land, new hope for the future of younger generations and a living testimony to the saving power of Jesus Christ.

For the older person, here is the wonder of forgiveness for a lifetime of sinfulness, a peace in the storm, a friend in loneliness, a comforter in lostness and bereavement. Here is the sure hope of an eternity with God as death approaches. Older people are often delightfully gregarious, and the church has so much to offer by way of friendship, fellowship and support – which works both ways, as an older person gives these in return. One of the joys of having older people in a church fellowship is that they have time to share and love to give. From a purely selfish point of view, we can be blessed by older folk being the quasi-grandparents, great-aunts and -uncles, to those of us who still rush round doing all the busy things needed in church and yet have a real need for those who have time to be our senior family.

Plan

I would want to encourage anyone, of any age, to feel they can be involved in sharing the good news of Jesus with those in their later years. Here is a special challenge from one leader of older people, Rhena Taylor: 'Often would-be evangelists to the elderly are elderly themselves.'[6] This means that we older ones need not to be backward in coming forward in our fellowships when it comes to what can be done by our church and, in a similar vein, should have courage to be those who share their own faith on a one-to-one basis. Let me explore this in a little more detail.

What can we do together? London City Mission has done some research here and produced a very good pamphlet called 'Reaching Out to the Elderly'[7]. They write of the value of advertising events run by the church that apply specifically to older people, making sure the print is large and readable, including in any invitation the offer of lifts and how they can be obtained. Posters work well – in day centres, newsagent windows and doctors' surgeries. They rightly encourage services in care homes, which will be considered in Chapter 13. They suggest lunch clubs and tea afternoons, which I have always found work really well. We all love food and good company, and a sensitive talk from someone who knows how to speak specifically to an older audience can be an ideal way of sharing the Gospel.

London City Mission is keen on the idea of what is known as 'Holidays at Home', an enthusiasm shared by many churches around the country, not least Winchester Baptist Church, whose members have produced their own instruction booklet[8]. This book can only give a few pointers, so it is worth contacting both of these sources for fuller details. I have seen holidays at home, and they are potentially brilliant. Instead of taking folk away, some of whom could not travel far anyway, a church turns its premises into a holiday site for a week. With plenty of imagination, much can be done. There could be world travel: a different country each day, different foods, crafts, music and so on. Or you could travel in time, taking in the different decades lived through by your older holidaymakers, again with appropriate pictures, music and food. There can be craft work, trips out, speakers and singers; the possibilities are vast. I would encourage a presentation at the Sunday services, where the excitement of the week can be shared, crafts displayed and food shared. The hard work and detailed preparation will be worth all the effort when you see the joy on so many faces and realize that some will have come to know Jesus through the friendship they have experienced and the message they have heard. This could then be continued on a monthly basis as a 'seniors messy church', so they can bring their friends and keep up their newfound friendships.

A concern would be how the Christian talk might go. Pilgrims' Friend Society has a very good little book of talks, *Sharing the Good News of Jesus*, subtitled *Epilogues and Talks with Seniors*, which is a good resource.[9] The key here is to speak with love and compassion, looking at the potential for our later lives, sharing God's love for older ones seen in the life, death, and resurrection of Jesus, telling how God gives new lives for old and the wonder of eternal life. It is worth re-reading Chapter 8 to see Scripture passages and themes that have helped those who are older to find faith.

There is no reason why a church should not have outreach services designed specifically for older people. I have always tried to include these in missions I have led. Songs of Praise rarely fails, with loved hymns interspersed with readings, prayers, a testimony from a senior and a well-pitched talk. This is often better held on a day other than Sunday, usually during daylight hours and followed by a lunch or tea. An annual service for those who have been bereaved is much appreciated, giving time for reflection, to give thanks and hear of God's care and grace.

It's not that there is nothing we can do together, the problem is that we do not sit down and work it out, we do not think 'older evangelism'. Let's have the courage to change our mindset and seek, as churches, to reach out to the many who live around our worship centre who, in their older lives, need Jesus so much.

Person to person

Whether or not the church collectively will do anything, there is nothing to stop us sharing our faith one to one. Or is there? Why is it so hard to share what we know to be true and enjoy in our own lives with those around us? Allow me to help you overcome your fears. The secret is knowing what you are doing and how you are doing it. Half a dozen 'know hows' and you can do it. Here they are:

1. Know your subject. Some of my grandchildren are learning French. They will soon realize that Grandpa does not know everything, but I would hate to disillusion them too soon, especially as I drink from a mug which proclaims 'Greatest Grandpa'. At present, I can converse with them in French because of a special reason: I have had to preach in French on my several visits to Niger in West Africa, a former French colony where the language is still spoken. It involved a lot of very hard work, but my mastery of that language, while not sensational, is passable. I am ahead, just, of my grandchildren right now.

A major problem in faith sharing is that we simply do not know our subject well enough. In a very keen and committed congregation, I did a series of talks on how we can chat with others about Jesus. I asked for complete honesty in answering the question, 'How many verses of the Bible do you know by heart, including chapter and verse?' Pretty much everyone made one, as we quoted together John 3.16. Everyone had to keep their hands raised if they knew two verses, as we recited Revelation 3.20. Slowly, hands went down as we raised the number. By ten verses, only three hands remained in the air, including the minister. How did these enthusiastic Christians hope to share their faith when they did not even know ten Bible verses?

Paul tells his friend Timothy that he is to be a 'workman who does not need to be ashamed', as he 'correctly handles the word of truth' (2 Timothy 2.15). Some homework may be needed here. The best bits of the Bible and the most effective verses are the ones that helped you and blessed your life. These are the ones to learn, so you feel confident in what you are saying. That said, do not let your apparent ignorance be a stumbling block. When Philip came to follow Jesus, he brought his friend Nathaniel to meet Jesus within a day of coming himself. When Nathaniel asked an impossible theological question, he gave a three-word answer: 'Come and see' and it worked (John 1.43–46). When someone becomes a Christian, their enthusiasm can be infectious, and lack of knowledge need be no barrier to their giving away their faith to a friend. In the same way, the woman who met Jesus as he was sitting beside a well went at once to tell her neighbours about her amazing encounter, so that many in the town trusted him for themselves, as John describes in Chapter 4 of his Gospel.

While ignorance need not be a hindrance, knowledge can be gained; the Bible is a great book and even a good working relationship with John's Gospel and some of the brilliant verses in it will work well. Try these: John 1.12, 1.29, 3.3, 3.16–17, 6.37, 8.34,36, 10.9–11, 10.27–28. That should do for starters!

2. *Know your person.* To barge in on someone with an 'Are you saved?' is a course I would advise against. Being a friend first is a much better idea. This is especially so with one in their later years. A simple 'Hello' in the local shop, an invitation to coffee or tea, a chat on a summer day over the garden fence – all build bridges and relationships. Your neighbours, friends and family are not fools; they know that you are one of those 'religious' people. They notice your going off to church on a Sunday. They may or may not want to know of your faith, but a pushy style will most likely put them off. Our aim should be to get to know our older friend or neighbour, so that our Christian life comes into a conversation quite naturally.

A real interest in an older person will include a great deal of listening. This may bring some very surprising results, as we learn of their life, which may well include their early experiences of the Christian life. Many older people were once churchgoers and probably went to Sunday school. Their reason for dropping out may not have been any overt hostility; it was more that lots found life too busy, families too demanding or leisure activities took over. I do not assume that I will face antagonism. For some, the church or its members behaved badly, and I have learned not to justify perceived wrongs, but to sympathize. It may well be that there has been a real faith, which now lies dormant and can be gently fanned back to life. This is a considerable advantage, to be compared with the increasing difficulty of having to start much further back in how those of younger generations need to explain the Christian faith almost from scratch to their contemporaries, who, by contrast, have no history with the Church or Christian beliefs at all.

Whatever we do, a kindly give and take, a genuine interest and a care for our neighbour or friend will prove to be the best way forward as we try to be faithful to our Christian witness.

3. *Know your Saviour.* You may feel this should have come first – and you may be right! But I saved it until now to make this point: we can have all the knowledge in the world and still make a mess of our faith-sharing unless we are really close to Jesus. He said to his first followers, as he was about to ascend into heaven, 'You will receive power when the Holy Spirit comes on you, and you will be my witnesses' (Acts 1.8). It is wonderful to know this enabling by God. Although I have a long experience of preaching as an evangelist, I make it a constant practice to ask God to fill me again with his Spirit each time I speak. If I am giving several talks in a day, that will mean several prayers and several fillings. I then know that my words will be his words – and his words will be my words.

When I am in a personal conversation, I frequently find myself praying as I talk and listen, so that what is happening is a team effort. I also find that it helps to give personal examples of how God has come to me, helped me and changed me. Older people especially love life stories. We each have a unique one to tell. How God has met us, forgiven us, changed us, helped us and blessed us has a real impact on others, especially if we are older and our listener is older as well. When we older ones share this testimony story with younger ones, it can show a future and a hope to them, letting them see how God can do something similar in their lives. Never underestimate the power of a story that will be visible on your face as you tell it. That is what Jesus meant when he said we are his 'witnesses': a witness speaks of what they know personally.

If you know Jesus, you have a spiritual life that is not only worth living but worth telling. Do it with humility, admitting failings as well as sharing victories. Be sure to give the glory to the Saviour: 'Not I, but Christ' (Gal 2.20).

4. Know your time. This is key and will be a major reason why you need to know your Saviour and his Spirit leading and guiding you. Remember my experience in sharing with my dying neighbour, Basil, in the last chapter. There was that quiet nudge to take my New Testament with me and the certainty that this was the moment to urge this lovely man to put his trust in Jesus there and then. It would also be true to say that there have been times when I have felt a firm, restraining hand on my arm, urging me to back off. God's Spirit is brilliant in knowing when we should advance or pause. Be in time with him in every conversation, in every meeting.

For someone to become a Christian, it is truly about being born. Birth should happen at the right time. Having said that, as an evangelistic preacher, I assume it is time for someone in my congregation, so it would be exceptional if I did not make a call for response. I do accept that this comes through the gift of evangelism, given to some (Ephesians 4.11). For others, pastors especially, they have to 'do the work of an evangelist' (2 Timothy 4.5), and work is always hard. But we are all Jesus' witnesses, called to shine like stars for him (Phil. 2.15). My advice, if you are not sure, is to gently push ahead, until it becomes clear that the limit has been reached.

5. *Know your limitations*. Phew! Here is the best one, I hear you say. You may be right, as knowing we cannot do something is as crucial as knowing what we can do. What I mean here is this: sometimes we may be the wrong person to speak to a certain friend, neighbour or family member. With some family members, for example, anything said may be received with antagonism, and we set that person back in their need of God and, at the same time, spoil the happy relationship we share.

There are people who are very close to me with whom I am completely reactive; if they choose to raise anything of a spiritual nature in conversation, I will respond gently and positively. But I feel God's restraint on my being proactive, as that would be counterproductive. This does not stop me from praying fervently for them, or showing Christ's love by the way I behave towards them. I confess that I find this restraint very hard, but I have to rest in the Lord. I was chatting with a lovely couple, who are close friends, the day before I wrote this. They are continually concerned, even distressed, for their adult son, who is antagonistic to anything to do with Jesus. I remind them that Jesus loves their son even more than they do, as they have never died for sinners like him, but Jesus has. I often have to hear my own words when I think of some I love.

This does not mean that we are limited in such a way that we feel chained up in a prison. If, for example, I am asked about a recent preaching visit to somewhere in Africa, I do enthuse about what has happened. I do not feel I have only to speak of the monkeys I saw, but also of the wonderful things God has been doing. People know why I have been there and, if they ask the question, I will give a happy but straight answer. They can make of it what they will; I did not preach at them, I shared my life's experience. It is a delicate balance, I know. What an exciting way to live!

6. *Know how to help.* To become a Christian is not an impossible task. It is a simple coming together of a sinful soul and a welcoming and forgiving Saviour. If you have the joy of being there when this happens to someone, your privilege is to be the enabler. It may be said by some that what follows is simplistic, and there is some merit in that observation. What I am trying to do is give an easy-to-remember guideline, which inevitably has its limitations, but here it is.

Every person who becomes a Christian does three things. They admit their need of Jesus, they believe he can meet that need and they then commit themselves to him, realizing that this is a life-changing and eternal commitment. You may have detected an ABC in there, so let me flesh that out.

There is an admission of need. In many of the guides you can read on 'How to lead someone to Christ', this 'A' is linked with words from Paul in Romans 3.23: 'All have sinned and fall short of the glory of God.' This is essential: we have to realize that we have got our lives wrong and that we need to be forgiven. In my experience, this is not necessarily where people start. Especially for older people, there are many more issues, and an admission of needing Jesus can come from various situations. For example, a remarkable number of people come to meet Jesus at a time of deep grief and bereavement, asking God to make true David's beautiful words, 'Though I walk through the valley of the shadow of death, I will fear no evil, for you are with me' (Psalms 23.4). Older people very often feel the burdens and weariness of life and want Jesus to take them and carry these hard things for them, as he so generously promises to do: 'Come to me, all you that are weary and burdened, and I will give you rest' (Matthew 11.28). Older people come to Jesus for various reasons, admitting their need; but that need does always have to have the element of sin that needs to be dealt with, or the next step is hopelessly devalued. The very first words of Jesus in his ministry are given by Mark: 'The time has come . . . The kingdom of God is near. Repent and believe the good news!' (Mark 1.15). We must turn from our sins, as well as turn to Jesus in our trust in him.

Here then is 'B': to trust Christ we believe that he is the one to whom we come. We are not coming into a religious system, or joining an organization called 'church' (although, without wanting to complicate what I am saying, new Christians will be part of the body of Christ, something crucial in being a Christian). No, we are meeting the Saviour, as he comes to meet us. As we admit our sins, we hear the echo of John the Baptist, as he pointed to Jesus and said, 'Look, the Lamb of God, who takes away the sin of the world.' When I started out, with an older translation, the word for 'Look' was 'Behold', which made it easy to remember, as it began with 'B', just as 'A' had 'Admit' coupled with 'All have sinned'. Little things like this nudge an ageing brain into being able to remember!

Lovingly, we bring the nearly Christian to see Jesus, who takes away our sin and carries our burdens as he dies on the cross. As Peter puts it, 'He himself bore our sins in his body on the tree' (1 Peter 2.24). For those who carry hurts and needs, 'Surely he took up our infirmities and carried our sorrows' (Isaiah 53.4) is a good one. I admit my need: Jesus meets that need.

It is still possible to agree with all this in theory, but do nothing about it. That is why there has to be a 'C', when we commit our lives unreservedly to Jesus as Saviour and Lord. Here is Matthew 11.28 again: 'Come to me,' says Jesus. We are so privileged now, as our response is to the risen and ascended Lord. His call needs a positive response, acknowledging that this will be life-changing and we will have a new Master for our lives and the power of his Holy Spirit living within us.

One thing is certain, the person with whom you are sharing this will not be able to grasp what all this means for their life. Tell them that you, yourself, are still trying to work out all the implications, but a simple step of repentance and trust is all they need, as Jesus will work it out for them and with them. With all his love, he has come to them. Now is the moment for a prayer of trusting commitment: help them with this, even suggesting what could be said. The prayer I use is in Chapter 8. It is a holy moment, so try to be in a quiet place, uninterrupted by any distraction. When they have prayed, you pray a prayer of thanks. But do not leave out the last 'Know how'.

7. *Know about assurance.* The New Testament is full of glorious certainty, and a new Christian needs to know the

truth and joy of this. When Jesus says he is knocking on the door, he promises that, if we hear and open, 'I will come in' (Revelation 3.20). The verb is strong and positive. To put it the other way round, 'I am the gate,' said Jesus, 'Whoever enters through me will be saved' (John 10.9). 'Whoever comes to me I will never drive away' (John 6.37) is another great verse of assurance. Find one you love and use it. An older person, having lived so long with a lack of faith, or with uncertainty, and living now amid the struggles of later life and with death nearer than it was, needs to be helped to be really sure that they are safe with Jesus.

I would not go much further than that at first. I would be making plans to share how prayer is such a blessing; how the Bible can become real, with good notes to help; how I could encourage this new Christian to enjoy fellowship and worship and, most of all, that I would be their close friend.

One final word on this subject: pray that God will give you the wonderful privilege of leading someone to Christ. Here is an old chorus I used to sing back in my youth:

Lead me to some soul today,
O teach me, Lord, just what to say;
Friends of mine are lost in sin,
And cannot find their way.
Few there are who seem to care,
And few there are who pray;
Melt my heart, and fill my life,
Give me one soul today.[10]

10
Hang on in there

In 1971, a Los Angeles photographer called Victor Baldwin produced a picture of a cat clinging on to a pole, under the title 'Hang in there, baby'. It became a cult hit, and he sold hundreds of thousands of prints. It was given to Vice President Spiro Agnew when he was forced to resign in 1973 and to President Richard Nixon after the Watergate scandal, which began in 1972. Johnny Bristol then wrote and recorded 'Hang On in There, Baby' in 1974[1], with many other artists using this for their own tracks, including Gary Barlow in 1998.[2]

The whole concept of the original photograph and the subsequent records was to say to the viewer or listener, 'Don't quit'. It is a sad fact that there are those who, in their later lives, do not heed these words as Christians and decide to give up. I was talking with a minister from somewhere in the South West of England who had been visiting homes in the villages around his church, to encourage people to share in their worship. He related how he had gone to one house, where the reception had been very frosty. The man told my friend that he had no desire to be part of any church. Pressed for a reason for his antagonism, he replied that he had had enough of church life – he himself had been a minister and that was enough. At another house it was even worse. 'I've done my time,' was the response. 'I'm through with Christianity.' This man had been a bishop, no less.

My friend, as may be imagined, was horrified. How could these two leaders in the church turn their backs on the faith they had once taught? Perhaps it was not their faith, but their involvement with church that was the problem, but their teachings would have included the need for fellowship and worshipping together. Clearly, it is possible to become an outright hostile apostate, but many more grow tired with their faith or, at least, their practice of it. Some fear that loved ones have died outside the Christian faith and, with the fear of being separated from them after death, determine not to go to heaven without them. This is surely tragically short-sighted, as God alone is the Judge and no one can say for certain about anyone else. There may be a resentment of church styles or practices, leading to a falling away from fellowship. The most difficult problem is when we fall apart physically or mentally and this impacts us spiritually. One of my closest friends has gone through the most grievous experience that has all but taken his faith. Such is his leadership in the church that I will call him 'Jack', although his friends will know about whom I am writing. In his late seventies, Jack was struck down with a sudden physical pain, resulting in his being prescribed some very aggressive painkillers in hospital, where he lay overnight in a cold room, frozen stiff. With a serious delirium, he felt as if the roof was caving in. No one could find where his infection was; he was taken off one type of painkiller but went through a fortnight he described to me as 'hell'. He was convulsed in tears and felt absolutely lost, crying out in the words of Psalm 13.1, 'How long, O Lord? Will you forget me forever?'

If Jack's suffering had lasted for that fortnight and then improved, I would not be writing his story. But it went on and on, for months on end. It was said that the drugs had affected his emotional state, and the forecast was that he might go on feeling as he did for up to a year. It needs to be appreciated that this is one of the finest Christian leaders I have ever known, a planter of churches, an influential speaker and Christian advisor to many, myself included. Yet here he was, crying out in the night to God, again from Psalm 13.1 'How long will you hide your face from me?' At his lowest points, Jack told me how he would literally cry out, getting up and pacing the garden at 3 a.m. so as not to disturb his wife, who was, understandably, going down as well.

Knowing his Bible well, Jack said how he felt like John the Baptist, questioning Jesus as to who he was (Matthew 11.3), and like Paul with his 'thorn in the flesh' (2 Corinthians 12.7), these verses seared in his memory. For Jack, one of the tragedies, as he came to see, is that many are tormented in similar ways and yet these deep problems are rarely addressed by ministers, and trite answers are so easily given. He confesses he as a preacher and leader had been guilty here. But to have to get up after lying in bed for only a few minutes, as many as 20 times in a night, was exhausting physically and mentally, never mind spiritually. He would read verses such as Isaiah 41.10, 'Do not fear, for I am with you, do not be discouraged, for I am your God' and literally hold out his right hand and cry 'God, hold me.'

After a whole year of going through this sense of lostness, Jack still has bad moments. He has been back to the medical experts, has seen psychologists about cognitive behavioural therapy and yet the lostness often returns. The problem with being a lifelong Bible teacher is that you know all the answers in your head. The verse about 'The peace of God, which transcends all understanding' (Philippians 4.7) was there in his knowledge, but not in his experience. 'My God will supply all your needs' (Philippians 4.19) was well known to Jack, but, as he told me, 'in the middle of the night it didn't feel that way.'

I am not telling this story to cause despair, but to show the agonies anyone can go through in their later life when something goes drastically wrong. I am happy to report that Jack is coming out of this dark tunnel. Although he has been desperate, having never known anything like it, he is learning again to simply trust the God who is always there, even in the deepest darkness. He told me how he has lost his brashness and self-confidence and said a very wonderful thing: 'You cannot affect the things that come to you in life, but you can affect the way you handle them.' Only by Jack's determination to look to God for his grace has he found a way through. 'May my prayer come before you; turn your ear to my cry,' pleads the writer of Psalm 88.2. For all who relate to Jack's story, it is a precious prayer. Jack said how vital his supportive wife and family were, and how valued were caring and praying friends. Many of us sometimes just have to 'hang on in there', as this chapter's title says.

Andrew is one of our local church leaders where I live, and he reminded me of a time, a few years ago, when the church was struggling with its unhelpful minister who gave people little support. Andrew told me how vital it was, then and now, to have a group of close Christian friends with whom he could meet for fellowship, prayer and mutual encouragement. 'You need good support when the going gets tough,' he says. 'You need supply lines for spiritual and practical help to keep you going.' Andrew was also grateful for a regional leadership that supported these local Christians through their difficult months and even years.

These are wise words; if we are to get through times of hardship, whether in our churches or our own lives, we need to have built around us a network of support, which will be there when everything seems to fall apart. I had a friend who was treated very badly by a Christian organization for whom she worked. Things became so bleak that she told her close friends, 'I've lost my faith.' They gave a beautiful reply: 'Don't worry. We will hold your faith for you and give it back to you when you are ready.' In the course of time, they did just that, and this lovely lady is now restored. There are echoes here of Moses growing weary in his prayers for Joshua, when Aaron and Hur hold up Moses' arms (Exodus 17.8–13). We need to be there for each other in times of trial, and when there is no one else there, as sometimes happens to me in the middle of the night, I have a little wooden 'holding cross' by my bedside, and I cling to it. I do not regard this as superstitious, but see it as a physical reminder of the love of Jesus in my darkest hour.

When life seems too hard to bear, we need to come back to the creedal principles of our faith and be reminded of the basics once again. I personally draw strength from words in 1 John 5.11–13:

This is the testimony: God has given us his eternal life, and this life is in his Son. He who has the Son has life;

he who does not have the Son of God does not have life.
I write these things to you who believe in the name of
the Son of God so that you may know that you have
eternal life.

Having trained to be, and practised as, a lawyer, I tend to
home in on the legal terms in the Bible. I was in court most
days, calling witnesses to give 'testimony' to the truth of
what they knew. Alas, too often I would hear what turned
out to be a false testimony, as people would lie through their
teeth! I am so glad that, these days, I represent only one
client, the Lord Jesus Christ, who always tells me the truth
so that, as I live and preach, his word is totally trustworthy
and sure. How vital this is in times such as Jack and Andrew
have gone through; God's word is constant and steadfast,
whatever our own circumstances.

What is this 'testimony'? It is that 'God has given us
eternal life.' What a relief to know that it is not my efforts,
or even my faith, that gains the assurance of a life that is
forever and therefore will never fail, even when my life is
struggling – but that it is God's gift. My certainty is not on
the vagaries of my circumstances, but on the rock-solid love
and mercy of a loving heavenly Father. When life is at its
worst, I rest in the fact of eternal life as the best thing I can
have; as William James famously said, 'The greatest use of
life is to spend it on something that will outlast it.'[3]

John gives us an even greater reason for our certainty of
faith, whether in good times or bad, as we get older: 'This
life is in his Son.' Of all the people who have ever lived, no
one can hold a candle to 'the light of the world' (John 8.12).

Here is assurance of the highest order: this is the one who has died and risen again, who holds 'the keys of death and Hades' (Revelation 1.19). Jesus has brought eternity to our world and our lives. My trust is in him. Because I belong to him, as John goes on in the verses quoted, 'He who has the Son has life.'[4]

Jesus himself was strong and clear on this: 'Because I live, you also will live' (John 14.19). Life is in Jesus. My fears, troubles, disasters and especially my doubts are wrapped up in his protection. From childhood until now, my favourite Bible verses have always been John 10.27–28:

> My sheep listen to my voice; I know them, and they follow me. I give them eternal life, and they shall never perish; no one can snatch them out of my hand.

There is no safer place to be than in the hand of the Lord Jesus Christ. In my older life, I have re-read these verses and realized something even more amazing, for Jesus goes on to say this in verses 29 and 30:

> My Father who has given them to me, is greater than all; no one can snatch them out of my Father's hand. I and the Father are one.

It is like a pair of hands, clasped together, with me in the middle. That really is safe! In my worst moments, even if I struggle to believe it or feel it in my heart at the time, God's protection is there. Sometimes we want to believe, but our circumstances mitigate against our feeling it to be so. This is not a unique experience; even the early Christians felt that way. John understands this and after his great affirmation of faith, tells his readers,

> I write these things to you who believe in the name of the Son of God, so that you may know that you have eternal life (verse 13).

It is wonderful when we have that inner conviction of God's presence, when 'The Spirit himself testifies with our spirit that we are God's children' (Romans 8.16). But, in those times when we do not 'feel', we can still 'know'. We, of course, have to be those who belong to Jesus because, as John cautions, 'He who does not have the Son of God does not have life' (verse 12). If that is the problem, then a re-visit of this book's Chapter 8 would seem advisable right now. Paul's stirring words are for those who know Jesus and are there for us older ones as life seeks to crush us:

> For I am convinced that neither death nor life, neither angels nor demons, neither the present not the future, nor any powers, neither height nor depth, nor anything else in all creation, will be able to separate us from the love of God that is in Christ Jesus our Lord (Romans 8.38-39).

Our salvation is assured. I have been so heartened to meet those who are even older than I am who are enduring to the end, despite their hardships. We need to see that we can not only 'hang on in there', but we can really thrive, however old we are. I am challenged, as well as enthused, when

I think of my own aunt, now over 90. Daphne is one of the loveliest people I know who, despite the various trials that beset many in their very older days, is constantly joyful. As I will explain, my conversation with her was unusual, so I had prepared some specific questions, rather than a general chat. As we began, my aunt said a lovely thing: 'In later life you grow in your trust of Jesus; it is important and I just want to do it.' As she spoke, her eyes welled up with tears; it was a very moving start to our conversation. It would be wrong of me to reveal some of the crosses she has had to bear, but my first question was this: 'How have you grown spiritually, and why is your faith stronger, with all the hurts you have had?' She replied thus: 'It is only by faith that you can know God's comfort and peace. In your sorrows, worries and anxieties, faith just grows.' Knowing the several hardships my aunt has gone through, this was a brave answer. It reminded me of the amazing thing Robert Murray M'Cheyne said in a letter dated 9 March 1843:

> You will never find Jesus so precious as when the world is one vast howling wilderness. Then he is like a rose blooming in the midst of the desolation, a rock rising above the storm.

The reason I was doing a 'question and answer' session was because, slowly but surely, Daphne has become profoundly deaf, so she now has an ingenious little microphone and handset that takes my words and prints them on the screen for her to read. She then speaks and I reply, she reads, and so on. I asked her how she can worship when church is silent to her. 'I've been there 70 years, and I've got used to many vicars,' she replied with a twinkle in her eye. 'The latest is a young man (which could mean anything when you are almost 90!) who gives me a personal full copy of his notes so I can follow his sermon (what a great idea!) People from church give me lifts; they are patient with my deafness and sit by me at church, scribbling down things like the notices. I follow the hymns and readings in the books.'

I had to ask what was probably the hardest question. It had, throughout my life, been a one word duo: 'DouglasandDaphne'. They were inseparable until his death, ten years ago.

'So, dear Daphne, were you angry when Douglas died, you being so close?'

'I asked for God's peace. I'm fortunate to have two children and other family. I certainly did not blame God. Everyone has this problem and you can't expect to have no problems; it's just part of being a human being. Your heavenly Father helps you deal with it.'

With all these answers being so strong, I could not help saying to Daphne that perhaps some of her attitude was a result of the old saying 'What goes around comes around.'

'Daphne, you and Douglas always looked after others, in your neighbourhood and at church: is that why others now look after you?'

'Yes, I suppose so. My daughter-in-law's mum is an amazing help; she makes sure I know what's happening. She's one of my scribblers! The neighbours are good, too.

And,' she added, 'there are worse things for the elderly – dementia, arthritis, being in a wheelchair with MS . . .'

Tell me I am biased if you will. But I left Daphne that day with a feeling that I had been with one of God's special older ones — a lady who had a completely positive approach to her whole life and so firm as she spoke about her certain faith in Jesus Christ, whom she had trusted, with Douglas, in their young married life and had gone on with that relationship, known her heavenly Father and continuing even more strongly into her late old age. Compared with her, I know I am in the early stages of ageing. If God spares me until I am over 90, I want to grow into it as she has done.

I had a similar reaction when I met Margaret and Ronnie, who are ahead of me by ten years, who gave the answers as to how Daphne does it, because they shared their secrets of growing old successfully as Christians. 'We keep faithful by our daily Bible reading and praying together,' was their first response when asked how they managed to stay the course in their Christian lives. 'It's good to attend a place of worship, and we never miss Sunday morning and evening.' Margaret was very happy that she had been in the choir 'ever since I've been able to sing'. She particularly mentioned one of the special pieces, which always spoke to her heart. From time to time her choir will perform Mendelssohn's 'Elijah', and there is a man she remembers singing, when she was a teenager, 'He that shall endure to the end shall be saved.'[5] (based on the sayings of Jesus in Matthew 10.22 and 24.13).

For Margaret, this has been a lifelong challenge. 'When I trusted Christ at eleven, I knew God had taken all my sin,' she told me. 'But I did sin more! The Lord touched my life deeply in 1984, so I knew he is with me every day. Nothing is too hard for him and I look to him for his strength.' Ronnie is a man of few words: 'Nothing will put me off now,' he quietly added. Margaret and Ronnie work on the same principles as Daphne, not only in their private devotions but in their corporate involvement. If the church provides help for older people, they are in on it: the midweek services and prayer meetings, with their fellowship and 'good craic' (they live in Northern Ireland). There is a Saturday morning prayer meeting for Margaret, followed by coffee and time for a hairdo. Their spiritual life is an integral part of all their life.

Surely here lies the way to keep on keeping on. Older age is no time for giving up when, with a deep relationship with Jesus and a continuing involvement with God's people, we can go right on to the end. Age magnifies our weaknesses because our end is nearer. We need to see the Lord's goodness, as we look forward to that day when we will be 'lost in wonder, love and praise.'[6]

Which brings me to a final conversation to share on this subject of keeping on, which will lead into the following chapter, as this chat was partly about facing death. I have known Cyril and Liz for over fifty years, ever since they came over from Ireland to lead the groundbreaking Catacombs coffee bar and youth centre in Manchester in the late sixties. Their never-fading faith, their indefatigable enthusiasm for Jesus and their varied roles in church leadership have been an inspiration. During the Vietnam war, as others looked on, they got active, helping many orphans find new homes over here, adopting one themselves and, in Cyril's case, being awarded the MBE for so doing. Together, they initiated very many projects to further the cause of Christ across Ireland. Liz was ordained, and their ministry together continued beyond retirement. To the horror of their family and friends, Liz fell victim to Motor Neurone Disease (MND). If ever there was a test of faith in later life, this was it. After a protracted illness, she died in June 2017.

We will meet Liz again shortly, but for this current chapter, Cyril is the man to answer the question: where was God in all this and how can a person cope when the love of their life is taken in such a cruel way when you are nearly 80? Is this not a time for kicking the Christian faith into touch (Cyril was a great rugby player)? The answer has to come in two phases: the period leading up to Liz's death and then Cyril's life alone. How did the two of them get through the steady and horrible decline of Liz's health?

'Until Liz was diagnosed with MND, neither of us had ever thought of growing old,' he told me. 'For us, there was no such thing as retirement. We were not going to be influenced by the world's "I did my job, paid my taxes." So, when Liz allegedly retired, she went to minister at a church in Southern Ireland in her late sixties, with me now in my early seventies.' By her third year, the diagnosis came, the biggest challenge ever for both of them. From the very start, Cyril said, there was never a question as to 'why me?' nor any self pity. They were keenly aware of the physical incapacity Liz would face, and they determined to go through everything with God's grace. A key to all this was to look at the book of Job and, like that brave man, to ask the same question he did: if God was there in the good times, does he change because of a medical diagnosis, or does he know what he is doing?

In a singular way, Cyril and Liz grew closer than ever before. Their two separate ministries merged into one. They came to terms with MND quickly. Cyril never gave up hope that Liz could be restored, accepting that this might not happen, as he told me, 'this side of glory'. Wisely, Liz insisted that Cyril keep up his interests, singing in the church choir, maintaining his circle of friends, going out for coffee. For her part, Liz saw this as a wonderful opportunity for a new area of Christian service. When friends came round to comfort her, she would turn the tables to find how they were – even when, towards the end, she was in a nursing home, she would minister to the nurses.

The whole point of this story, for me, is that we do have a choice. We can either give in, roll over and die, or we can make the conscious choice Liz and Cyril made, to let their faith grow and deepen and find new openings to live for Jesus and share his good news with others in a way that is unique to suffering. The email that came in June 2017 had these few words: 'At three a.m., Liz went home.' That was it. She had carried right on through.

So to the second phase: what about Cyril's Christian life after that, as he approaches 80 all on his own, without the love of his life? This was part two of my questions with Cyril, as we sat together in his home one Saturday morning in late 2017.

'I know whom I have believed' was how he started this part of our conversation, echoing Paul's comment to

Timothy (2 Timothy 1.12). 'Liz has been healed on the other side, in heaven.' I naturally agreed, but said that that did not really deal with him in the here and now. Cyril responded with a very honest remark: he and Liz had lived off each other's experiences, but after her death, his dependency had to shift much more to relying on God, not on her. 'She could have been my crutch,' he admitted. 'Now, I have to have my own spiritual walk with God, and this is now developing much more intimately.' Even now, Cyril is not questioning God, grateful for all his many friends and brilliant family, and 'staying blessed'.

I know good Christian people who do not react in this way and do not 'hang on in there'. Cyril has chosen a tough way, but a way with God. He is not pretending this is easy – 'the weekends are hardest,' he confessed. 'They were our special times.' There is this vacuum of no soulmate, no one to tell him they love him, which he misses deeply. There is no one to ask, 'is this tie alright?' – no one to tell him he is sniffing with a cold, no one to whisper to him. He admits to an over-whelming sense of loss as he walks through the valley of the shadow of death. All this, he told me, is Satan's attempt to have a go, when the victory of Christ has been won. And Satan will not be allowed to win, not in Cyril's life.

Cyril and Liz, and the others who have helped me pen this chapter, throw down the challenge: are we going to end our race well or fall at the final hurdle? We may feel we are deserted by God, as Job did, but a quiet reading of his re-markable story will show how he came through and was rescued and restored by God. This is the God who says to us,

> Let him who walks in the dark,
> Who has no light,
> Trust in the name of the Lord
> And rely on his God (Isaiah 50.10)

I will come back to this theme in the very last chapter of this book, when I look at Paul's stirring words from 2 Corinthians 4.16–18, telling us that 'We do not lose heart.' Life is a balance, with good times to be remembered as we 'number our days aright' (Psalms 90.12). This is no time to quit. This is the time to go with Jesus and to know he is there every step of the way, even to death: which is what we face on the next page.

11
Feel the fog

Lurking between Alexander Solzhenitsyn's *August 1914* and Matthew Henry's *Commentary in One Volume* on my bookshelves is a third rather ancient hardback book, Edward Gibbon's *The Decline and Fall of the Roman Empire*, abridged by D.M. Low.[1] Gibbon took 12 years to write this in no fewer than six volumes. It crossed my mind to write about our twenty-first century lives as a 'decline and fall', with an end perhaps not as dramatic or climactic as that of the Roman Empire, but nevertheless falling down all the same. Attend a non-religious funeral, and it certainly feels that way. Is that the way those of us who are Christians have to approach death?

The opening chapter of this book has shown my love for the poetry of Robert Browning and these first lines of 'Prospice' gave me an infinitely better title for this current chapter:

Fear death? – to feel the fog in my throat,
The mist in my face,
When the snows begin, and the blasts denote
I am nearing the place.

Browning looks at the challenge of his own death and includes the lines:

I was ever a fighter, so – one fight more,
The best and last!
I would hate that death bandaged my eyes, and
    forbore,
And made me creep past.
No! let me taste the whole of it . . .
O thou soul of my soul! I shall clasp thee again,
And with God be the rest![2]

Let us dare to 'feel the fog' and face death head on, as we look at our own death, that of others, and discover the Jesus way.

A death sentence

Students of English will agree that 'a death sentence' is not a 'sentence' but a 'phrase'. However, death itself is also not a 'sentence' or, at least, it does not need to remain that way. It begins that way for all of us, since 'the wages of sin is death' (Rom. 6.23). But even death itself is redeemed for the believer. One thing is sure, death is inevitable. 'Man is destined to die once,' proclaims Hebrews 9.27. Death and the process of dying are to be found in the Bible nearly a thousand times.

> We have harnessed millions of pounds, vast technology, incredible scientific progress, stunning medical understanding to keep us alive for as long as possible. However, there is no invention to stop us from dying.[3]

So says Ann Clifford at the beginning of her book *Time to Live*. 'Flight is an option, but we cannot outrun death,'[4] is her later observation. 'Death is not a failure. Death is normal,' says Atul Gawande[5]. 'Life is a risky business whose outcome is always fatal',[6] Robert McCrum tells us in his book *Every Third Thought*, which gets its title from Shakespeare's 'The Tempest', where Prospero says that 'every third thought shall be my grave.'[7] As Shakespeare says, this is something of which we are all aware; we all think about it. It affects us all. John Wyatt has written a powerful book, *Matters of Life and Death*, where he says:

> Death and dying are not just 'out there' as abstract theoretical issues. Death is here in our midst. You, the reader, carry your future mortality with you as you read these words. To be a little over dramatic, I am writing as a dying man to dying people.[8]

Wyatt is right; we are all in there. The opening words of Stephen Levine's book *Who Dies?* are: 'Today, approximately 200,000 people died,'[9] while Henri Nouwen makes that personal: 'People are dying. Not just the few I know, but countless people everywhere, every day, every hour.'[10] Try as we might, we cannot escape this fact, even if, with Woody Allen, we jokingly say, 'I'm not afraid of death; I just don't want to be there when it happens.'[11] The incomparable Louis Armstrong, in his song 'Cabaret', tells us that it is a short journey from our birth to our death.[12]

Are we ready? Many are not, at least for the possible imminence of death. Henri Nouwen, in his book about dying, writes this:

While sitting alone in my little hermitage, I realize how unprepared I am to die. The silence and the solitude of this comfortable apartment are sufficient to make me aware of my unwillingness to let go of life. Nevertheless, I will have to die soon. The ten, twenty, or thirty years left to me will fly by quickly.[13]

Be careful of making such a prediction: within two years of writing these words Nouwen died of a heart attack in the airport at Amsterdam, en route for Russia where he was to have made a documentary. Nouwen was a Christian writer, but the warning also comes from the secular writer Robert McCrum:

A self assured generation, which has lived so well for so long, is having to come to terms with a complex universal truth: make peace with death and dying, or find the inhibitions of everyday life in your final years becoming a special kind of torment.[14]

The prophet Amos puts it most starkly when he warns Israel of impending judgements: 'Prepare to meet your God' (Amos 4.12). Wonderfully, as Christians, we can face death not as a threat but as a promise. The voice of coming death does not have to be the voice of doom. Mary, a friend of mine in her nineties, wrote on her 2017 Christmas cards, 'Still on planet Earth, awaiting lift-off'! Billy Graham was quoted on the BBC on the day of his death, 21 February, 2018, 'Some day you will hear Billy Graham is dead: don't believe a word of it. I will have gone into the presence of God.' The New York Times, on the same day, quoted Graham as saying,

'I'm looking forward to that day when I'll see Christ face to face. Are you?'

Death can be feared or welcomed. Nouwen notes how we are fearful people, afraid of death more than anything else.[15] This is not unreasonable. Paul Tournier, a Christian doctor, says:

> Some anxiety will remain, conscious or not, especially in the face of death. And I believe that there is more peace to be found in the acceptance of human anxiety than in hope for a life or an old age freed from anxiety. Death remains a fearful and cruel monster. The Bible says that it will be the last enemy to be overcome (1 Corinthians 15.26).[16]

I do believe, personally, that this fear has an answer in Jesus, as I will seek to show shortly. I understand what Gratton and Scott are trying to say in their totally secular *The 100-Year Life* when they point to other ways of preparing:

> Drawing from economics and psychology, we have made the case that living longer requires a fundamental redesign of life and a restructuring of time. Only then can longevity be a gift and not a curse.[17]

Nevertheless, I am not at all convinced that 'economics and psychology' can in any way prepare us for our older years, and they can in no way prepare us for death. But at least they tell us to prepare! I much prefer Ann Clifford's response:

Fear of death is a natural fear. Whether we live with fear is a choice. God does not want us to live fearful lives. His peace, His grace and His kindness are available. The key question is – do you trust Him?[18]

How we approach death comes from deep within[19], as even secular writers know. PDM-2 puts it this way:

The subject of death may be faced in different ways by the elderly, depending on whether a person has attained a healthy self-integration or, conversely, has a terrifying sense of dispersion and loss of hope.[20]

Stephen Levine entitles one of his chapters 'Finishing business'.[21] I would want to underline again the value of getting the 'business' of approaching death sorted out. I do not have space here to deal with this in detail, but commend Ann Clifford's book *Time to Live*,[22] half of which she devotes to the practicalities with which we need to deal. Suffice to say that our getting ready for our own demise should include forgiving and being forgiven. This includes the need for reconciliation where relationships have gone wrong. We need to write the letters, make the telephone calls and pay the visits we never quite got round to. It is really important to write a will, so our family will not struggle with what to do with our possessions. As I will say later, the greatest preparation is to be at peace with God.

Another's death

Dealing with your own death is often massively easier than coping with another's. My wife and I lost our only daughter through a miscarriage. My mother and both my brothers died before they were 50. Speaking at my younger brother's funeral was, by far, the hardest talk I have ever had to give. My own book on bereavement was written as a result of great pains and hurts.[23] Billy Graham was splendidly upbeat about his own death, but he wrote of his wife's death:

> Although I rejoice that her struggles with weakness and pain have all come to an end, I still feel as if a part of me has been ripped out, and I miss her more than I ever could have imagined.[24]

He wrote that four years after his wife Ruth had died: clearly he had not got over it. Yes, she was safe with Jesus, but Graham still struggled. As the Bishop of Derry and Raphoe, Ken Good, said at the funeral of a mutual friend in 2017, 'Now we have the pain without the reason; in Heaven we will have the reason without the pain.' Never underestimate the impact of a bereavement, or attempt to speed up the grieving process. With a sudden loss there may well be a state of shock, with numbness of emotions. This may include a genuine denial: 'I don't believe it!' These are both inbuilt safety measures to get us through the first dreadful days, but need to be left behind as soon as possible. I realize this is almost contradicting my advice about not rushing through bereavement, but a serious shock can be physically and emotionally damaging, so an elongated period of this could need medical help. Hard though it may be, a funeral is a positive event.

Time is not necessarily a great healer, but time is needed for proper grieving. I agree with a friend who shared with me how we need to be allowed to weep and grieve. Christians often go for a 'thanksgiving service', full of jollity, which actually may militate against a proper time of grieving. Do we realize that a funeral is not for the deceased, as they are not there, but for us? We have got to say 'Goodbye', especially to our nearest and dearest. This is a cruel part of losing a partner or a child. I wrote earlier of Keith and his faithful service to God in his later life. He told me of his wife's death after her long suffering. The initial reaction, after he had told her to 'relax and trust' as she died, was to go into the next room and scream. Now time has moved on, and Keith said two very helpful things. 'You don't get over it, but you do come to terms with it,' he said. He has allowed his family and friends to be there for him, and for God to sustain him. But the other thing he said will find an echo with many. 'I have plenty of friends to do something with, but I have no one to do nothing with.'

There may be anger in bereavement and, sometimes, guilt. Both should be recognized, accepted and then brought to Jesus at his cross for help and forgiveness. As Keith has done, we need to allow others to help us and love us: this is no time for selfishness and pride in refusing what is offered. If we are helping someone who is bereaved, practical support often works better than too many words, as we show our love and comfort, make a few meals and be there to help.

I want to make a special plea: do not leave God out or turn from him at such a time. The absolute lostness without him is shown by McCrum's tragic words:

> Works of literature fill the void of faith, but in the end everything goes pear shaped. The best laid plans fail. Trust in good health gets betrayed. Futures go south. Rational projections spin awry; families implode. Chance, fate, old age, mortality and finally oblivion take over. Bereavement cuts through the hopes of the living like a scythe.[25]

McCrum's book, *Every Third Thought*, is deeply moving. It is matched by Julian Barnes' *Levels of Life*, which speaks powerfully of loss, summed up in these awful words after an especially terrible death: 'I do not believe I shall ever see her again. . . . Nor do I believe we shall meet again in some dematerialized form.'[26] In his grief, Barnes has a serious crack at well-meaning Christians, which we may not want to hear, but need to:

> I told one of the few Christians I know that she was seriously ill. He replied that he would pray for her. I didn't object, but shockingly soon found myself informing him, not without bitterness, that his God didn't seem to have been very effective. He replied, 'Have you ever considered that she might have suffered more?' Ah, I thought, so that's the best your pale Galilean and his dad can do.[27]

I do not dismiss this bitter criticism and confess my guilt at giving trite answers. It is better to agree with the Christian writer Louise Morse: 'We used to teach medical students that the four letter word in late life problems was "loss".'[28] Whoever the Christian was who spoke with Barnes about his wife's death should have heeded Dr Tournier's caution:

> Widowhood is always a terrible trial, and in addition to the emotional shock of separation there is always considerable disturbance in the social and personal life of the surviving partner.[29]

In my bereavements and those of others, I continually return to the splendid honesty of Psalm 23. In good and bad days, I both want and need to say 'The Lord is my shepherd,' so that I 'lack nothing'. I need him, very frequently, to 're-store my soul' and 'guide me' in the right paths. More than anything, I need to take on board those loveliest of words from verse four:

> Even though I walk through the valley of the shadow of death, I will fear no evil, for you are with me, your rod and staff, they comfort me.

I have come to understand a very special thing from David, that Psalm's writer, that the 'valley' may be that of 'death', but he says it is really 'the valley of the shadow of death'. Shadows only exist when there is light: we walk with Jesus and his light is always shining, even if all we see at the time is the darkness of the shadow. His way is best.

The Jesus way

As we 'feel the fog' of death, it is immeasurably reassuring to realize that Jesus himself has walked this way first. Cristi Murgu, the pastor of Carnforth Free Methodist Church, said in November 2017, 'Jesus lived with a diagnosis of death.' Of course, we cannot do what he did, but his example can be a guide for our living and dying. Jesus' death is unique. He died so that we do not have to die. We cannot die his atoning death. Nonetheless, he is also our example. We are to imitate him. And that includes in his dying. Dr David Field has preached on the seven 'words from the cross', showing how these can help us. I add my thoughts to his.

'*Father forgive them.*' We need to come to terms with those who have wronged us and talk with our heavenly Father about them, to give us a calm spirit. Seeking and giving forgiveness gives closure to wrongs received and done. This strikes at the very root of our being Christians. The Lord's prayer itself shows that our own forgiveness depends on our forgiving others, as Jesus pointed out specifically when he gave the prayer to his disciples (Matthew 6.12,14–15). To carry the burden of an unforgiving heart into our last days is to deprive ourselves of the peace we long to have at the last. If Jesus could forgive even those who were killing him, he can give us the strength and the ability to forgive those who have wronged us, however grievously.

'*Woman here is your son . . . here is your mother.*' As we come to our death, what a help and blessing it is to care for others, to put our affairs in order. I have written elsewhere in this book of the practical ways we can help, but this is a special gift we can give. Even as Jesus dies, he seeks to care for his mother and his best friend. This takes our care for our nearest and dearest beyond the practicalities: it is to ensure, as far as we are able, the wellbeing of our loved ones, to see that they are able to look after each other and be there, the one for the other when we are gone. It is a matter of the heart.

'*Today you will be with me in paradise.*' We have good news for others, bringing comfort and blessing. It is amazing to realize that, as Jesus is dying in great agony, bearing our sins, he has time to proclaim salvation to a condemned sinner. There is no cut-off point in our lives for faith-sharing. Our last days may give us a unique opportunity for a caring evangelistic word to those who are near us and who, because of our vulnerable state, may be especially open to God's call on their lives.

'*My God, why have you forsaken me?*' Being honest with God about our pain, confusion, loneliness and loss is allowed. The process of dying is clearly an agony for some. What a relief to see the way Jesus spoke here to his Father! In helping others who feel like this, we can reassure them with how Jesus cried out and that they are not in any way wrong to do the same. As the Father heard Jesus, so he hears us. When the process of dying seems unbearable, we can and must share this with God.

'*I thirst.*' Will we allow others to care for us? 'How can I help you?' is something we instinctively say to those in great need. There is no shame in responding with an answer which reveals our needs as we die. To say, 'I'm fine,' when we clearly are not, is not only unhelpful to ourselves, but hurtful to those who long to care. Jesus had a very practical longing for a drink and cried out for this need to be met. As a foreign soldier sprang to help, how much more will our family and friends come to our aid. Let us not deprive them of the very thing they long to do.

'*It is finished.*' Clinging to life is not as good as being ready to die. When all the forgivenesses have been given, when the caring is complete, the agonies past and the practicalities dealt with, there comes at last the time to let go. Life here does end. It is time to say 'Goodbye.'

'*Father, into your hands I commend my spirit.*' Like Jesus, we can trust ourselves confidently into our Father's arms. What a moment! We step through the curtain of our physical death into the immediate presence of our Lord and Saviour. May we do so in the beautifully quiet way Jesus did, with his help. What a blessing for us. What a blessing for those we leave behind. It is a privilege to have a good death.

I am extremely grateful for these thoughts from David. 'Blessed are the dead who die in the Lord' (Revelation 14.13). Because of Jesus, we can do this. As Christians, we rejoice that this leads to resurrection, for Jesus and, therefore, for us.

As Peter puts it:

God . . . in his great mercy has given us new birth into a living hope through the resurrection of Jesus Christ from the dead, and into an inheritance that can never perish, spoil or fade – kept in heaven for you (1 Peter 1.3-4).

This is a glorious hope, but we can only come to the resurrection via death. Because of the promised inheritance,

'Dying is a terrible mystery, but it is an opportunity for growth.'[30] As Ann Clifford points out:

> Finding faith in God who tenderly cradles us in our freefall from life can bring peace to the turmoil in which we find ourselves.[31]

What a contrast with those who do not share the Christian faith, shown in the way Stephen Levine concludes his book, *Who Dies?* Levine, a Buddhist, who died in 2016, refers to his faith-founding father the Buddha who, when dying, was asked by his followers what they should do to maintain their practice after he was gone. He replied, 'Be a lamp unto yourself.'[32] How glad I am that Jesus has come and said, 'I am the light' (John 8.12). My own light so often flickers, but his does not. As we follow the light of Christ on the journey to and through death, 'we are pilgrims on our way home.'[33] Billy Graham puts is like this:

> We were not meant for this world alone. We were meant for Heaven, our final home. Heaven is our destiny, and Heaven is our joyous hope.[34]

Despite the approach of death being often painful and in many ways frightening, this realization gives a joy which transcends all other emotions. Derek Prime, in his eighties, delightfully says of himself: 'In old age I am in the 'departure lounge', waiting for God's call home!'[35] Death should, ultimately, have no fear attached to it. I often quote, either in conversation or in prayer, when with someone who is facing an uncertain future, which could well include death, the stirring words of Romans 14.8:

> If we live, we live to the Lord; and if we die, we die to the Lord. So, whether we live or die, we belong to the Lord.

Here is something to get really excited about, from Paul's great triumphal outburst in 1 Corinthians 15.53–57:

> For the perishable must clothe itself with the imperishable, and the mortal with immortality. . . . then the saying that is written will come true: 'Death has been swallowed up in victory'. 'Where, O death, is your victory? Where, O death, is your sting?' The sting of death is sin, and the power of sin is the law. But thanks be to God! He gives us the victory through our Lord Jesus Christ.

These stirring verses from Romans and 1 Corinthians excite me greatly. As a Christian, I want to live in the light of what these truths proclaim: that death is beaten through Christ's death, and that eternal life is ours through his resurrection and ascension. Paul is right: we should not only 'live to the Lord', but know that our death is 'to the Lord'. The shout of triumph from the Corinthian verses should be for each of us a joy and a challenge to live well and die well. This was why Paul was able to say, as he faced his own death, 'For me to live is Christ and to die is gain' (Philippians 1.21). He knew that, because of the death and resurrection of Jesus, death itself had lost all its power.

I said at the beginning of this chapter that we would take on the subject of death and dying head-on, as it were. As I conclude, I would observe that Paul adopts exactly this approach, as I have just shown. He is constantly aware of his own mortality, but has no fear. In another stirring passage, he speaks of his confidence of going home to God. I commend a slow reading of 2 Corinthians 5.1–9, where he says how he is 'longing to be clothed with our heavenly dwelling' (v.2). The fog has lifted; the sunlight is with us.

Let me end this chapter with an amazing testimony. I wrote earlier about my friend Cyril and how he coped with the death through MND of his wife, Liz. If you can, you need to go on You Tube to see the video made by this brave lady as she approached death.[36] She speaks of wanting to glorify God through her death, calling her dying 'an expedition of faith' and pleading with her viewers, 'don't be lost.' Liz's humour balances with her seriousness, as she says:

> It is a great privilege to have a time factor. There is no cure for MND, except what God can do – I haven't thrown away the golf clubs. If there is no cure, I know God is able to carry me through.

In Liz's final months, before the MND took away her movement, she wrote a series of exquisitely crafted poems, now published in a book. Her very last one, written in November 2016, recalled times climbing in Ireland's mountains, as she faced her final climb from this life to the next. The last verse speaks of her assurance, which can be ours:

Look now – a different mountain up ahead!
Must I take that stony route instead?
Co-climber Christ beside me,
His Word and Spirit guide me
And hold me as I struggle to the summit
To conquer and confess that
He has done it.[37]

12

The long goodbye

It seemed hilarious at the time, as the President of the United States fluffed his lines. There he was, bodyguard at his right shoulder, ending an impromptu speech with the usual words, 'God bless . . .', at which point he dried up. 'America, Mr President,' the aide whispered, loudly enough for the microphone to catch the words. 'America', repeated the President, his smile never flickering. What a gaffe! How I laughed!

But it was no gaffe. When the truth came out later, I was ashamed of my mockery. For President Reagan was on the long road into dementia. In November 1994, he wrote, 'I now begin the journey that will lead me into the sunset of my life,' knowing he had the disease. His wife, Nancy, spoke at the Hotel Pierre in New York in July 1995:

> Alzheimer's is a disease, like any other disease – cancer, heart disease, whatever. But it is a really cruel disease, because for the caregiver (here her eyes reddened and her voice broke), it is a long goodbye.[1]

Just before Reagan died in 2004, Mrs Reagan said, poignantly, 'Ronnie's long journey has finally taken him to a distant place where I can no longer reach him.'[2] These two statements led Ken Johnson to write and sing 'The Long Goodbye',[3] which gave the title to this chapter.

I confess that this is the toughest chapter for me. I am not a medical practitioner, nor an expert on this most difficult subject. I am in awe of John Swinton, John Wyatt and Tom Kitwood, to mention only three of the many gifted and knowledgeable writers I will be quoting. After all my research, I am sure of one thing above all: God is the lover of our souls, whatever our condition, and we need to hear again the invitation from Jesus, 'Come to me, all you who are weary and burdened, and I will give you rest' (Matthew 11.28). Dementia is a big problem, but the love of God is greater.

Roger Hitchings, who has been speaking and writing with great expertise on this subject for many years, wisely said to me, 'Dementia is a huge subject, and no one can cover everything in a small volume.' My readers will have to go to his writings and those of the others I quote for more wisdom, but this chapter seeks to give some help in a field which is, often, a minefield.

The statistics are stark:

In rich countries dementia is becoming the major risk of ageing: one per cent of 60-year olds, seven per cent of 75-year olds and thirty per cent of 85-year olds have dementia.[4]

By age eighty-five, working memory and judgement are sufficiently impaired that forty per cent of us have textbook dementia.[5]

The commonest dementia, known as Alzheimer's, affects four per cent of all retired people and a fifth of the over 85's – about 700,000 Britons.[6]

These figures, from Gratton and Scott, Gawande and James, respectively, need two contrasting comments to put them in context, the first negative and the second more positive. John Swinton's brilliant *Dementia, Living with the Memories of God* quotes from a government poll, which showed that more people fear dementia (31 per cent) than cancer (27 per cent) and death itself (18 per cent). Among adults aged 30 to 50, 52 per cent fear that their parents will develop dementia, compared with 42 per cent fearing cancer and 33 per cent heart attacks. For retirees, 34 per cent worry about health, more than money at 33 per cent. In the health category, 52 per cent cited dementia, compared with 33 per cent cancer and 30 per cent stroke.[7]

Swinton follows these figures with a bleak remark: 'Cancer evokes concern; dementia evokes fear.'[8] I hear this, but would want to avoid hysteria. The vast majority will not get dementia: on the most bleak projections, a maximum among the oldest bracket of citizens will mean that over 60 per cent will die without dementia. Morse and Hitchings, both of whom have studied the subject deeply and have combined to write *Could It Be Dementia?* wisely say:

> It's worth mentioning that not everyone who reaches old age will develop dementia and not everyone who develops dementia struggles with fears and anxieties. Many become quite content and happy.[9]

Of all the subjects researched for this book, this is the one about which there is the most literature and where there appears to be the greatest divergence of views. Personally, I wrote this in an earlier book:

Alzheimer's Disease (after Alois Alzheimer, the German neurologist who first described this physical disease in 1907) is the most common form of dementia, a progressive disease causing inability to reason, think, learn and remember.[10]

Definitions from others vary. In conversation with Roger Hitchings, he spoke of dementia making the body malfunction, a disease which affects the brain and its memory, controlling the mind and dominating one's mental functioning. Sadly, everyone agrees with Oliver James, that 'there is no cure for Alzheimer's, nor any sign of one.'[11] As to what dementia actually is, Morse and Hitchings go back to the Latin, where the word 'means, literally, apart from, or away from the mind. It is one of the least understood conditions, and one of the most feared.'[12] Tom Kitwood takes this further, referring to other research sources to show that it refers to the whole person, not just the brain[13]. This is a brief summary from an author who takes an entire chapter to explain 'Dementia as a Psychiatric Category'[14]. Later in his book, he also speaks of how dementia needs to be seen as 'affecting the central nervous system, in which personality and identity are progressively destroyed', compared with more recent views that 'dementing illnesses should be seen, primarily, as forms of disability,' where how a person is affected 'depends crucially on the quality of care.'[15]

John Swinton, writing from his position as Chair in Divinity and Religious Studies at the School of Divinity, History and Philosophy at the University of Aberdeen, challenges many previous definitions of dementia in these statements:

> Dementia is the product of both damaged neurons and
> the experience of particular forms of relationship and
> community . . . Dementia has to do with more than
> neurology and neurological decline . . . Dementia
> doesn't entail a loss of mind. Rather it provokes others
> to presume that there is a loss of mind . . . Dementia
> doesn't entail a loss of self.[16]

I am trying not to do Swinton a disservice by selectively
quoting, but the major point he seems to make is to say this:
previous definitions of dementia see it as only a brain malfunction, or as a loss of mind or personality, whereas it is
much broader than that. He dares to argue, probably with
great justification, that what we assume (loss of mind) is not
always correct. I have to say that, in my limited experience,
I agree with his findings, and this colours what now follows.

If this were a medical treatise, we would be looking at the
various different types of dementia. That is not the point of
this book: I am looking at how we can age with God and
help those who have dementia to do this.

> The suggestion that a person has impaired thinking
> might be helpful for a psychologist, but it is much
> less helpful for a theologian with a critical eye on the
> implications of uncritically accepting such an obvious
> statement.[17]

Swinton's comment is vital. The question here is not whether a person is ill, because they obviously are, nor is it even
the exact nature of their illness. The greater question is this:

how we see the sufferer from a Christian standpoint – does it mean they are not 'human' anymore? Does Descartes' maxim, looked at earlier in this book, 'I think, therefore I am', mean that if I do not think, then I am not? How do we know if the person with dementia is thinking, but unable to communicate this? We cannot know for sure what is going on, even though brain scans can show deterioration, even a dying, within sections of the brain. Is Descartes right, or are we more than thinkers? I believe we are: we are eternal beings and, as such, are always of eternal value to God and, therefore should be treated as such. 'If anyone is in Christ, he is a new creation' (2 Corinthians 5.17). I will explore this in detail later in this chapter.

If we do not accept the inherent dignity of a human being, whatever their condition, we can descend to the dreadful words of McCrum:

> Deep in the cortex, the seahorse-shaped part of the brain, known as the hippocampus, creates humanity by processing a myriad external sensations, creating memory. Without memory, the human animal becomes, quite simply a brute beast deprived of character and personality.[18]

Dear, oh dear! This needs challenging on various fronts. We are not 'human animals'; we are created in the image of God (Genesis 1.26). Second, how does McCrum know if we ever lose our memories, just because we cannot express what we are thinking? Third, is 'memory' the only thing which makes us human? Where is 'the breath of life', which

God breathes into us (Genesis 2.7)? Louise Morse addresses a person with dementia:

> Your behaviour has changed – but have you? No, the essence of who you are, the person known to God, has not changed – you are the same 'you'. But the controls that you used to communicate with your world are becoming unreliable and, conversely, the same controls that fed you back information that made sense of your world are no longer working well, either.[19]

This has to be a wiser approach than McCrum's and needs to be taken to its obvious conclusion: just because these lines of communication seem to break down completely does not mean the person has become dehumanized, until their birth certificate is replaced by their death certificate. 'Behaviour changes, but personality does not', writes Graham Stokes.[20] Whatever we do, we must beware of concluding that the real person has gone, whatever the outward appearances show, especially in the later stages of dementia. Certainly, as this happens, it is frightening to watch, but the wise words of Swinton must be heeded: 'There is nothing that can occur to an individual that can make him less of a person.'[21]

When we accept this, it will help us deal with what is often very strange behaviour as a person slides into dementia. Andy's mother is in the later stages of frontal lobe dementia, where she now appears not to know him. Once a nervous, unsure lady, she now flirts with him, enjoys male company and speaks with a torrent of random words. She seems to have no understanding of prayer or spiritual recognition, or any memory of previous visits. Yet, says Andy, she seems never to have been happier, not afflicted by the pressures of life, including people, which often weighed her down as a vicar's wife. What is Andy to make of his mother?

In a similar vein, David has a friend Peter, a deeply prayerful man, with a love for his children, a joy in the Lord and a sparkle in his eyes. Now hospitalized after several strokes, his conversation is peppered with strong swear words, his behaviour toward the nurses is lewd and his temper alarming. David questions which of these two Peters is the real one and where he now is spiritually. David visits a care home to see Barbara, another lovely Christian lady, who now, in her demented condition, screams and assaults the care assistants giving her a shower. For David and Andy, these are challenging situations and are replicated in many who see lovely people change into almost unrecognizable opposites.

My sister-in-law, Judy, a highly qualified and experienced senior nurse, told me how, especially in Lewy body dementia, the whole personality changes. A committed Christian, Judy explained that, just because the sufferer cannot express or use their Christian faith does not mean that they never had, nor have not now, a real faith – it means that a change has happened. It is, she said, like a bookcase falling, where only some books remain upright. The person does not choose to be bad. Dr Jennifer Bute, herself with dementia, explained this further to me, saying the vile language was like suffering from Tourette's syndrome, where the sufferer cannot help their words. It is, she told me, like the hinges coming off a safety door. Our brains retain everything we have ever seen and heard, and the bad comes charging out. Stress increases the danger of this, when needs are not met.

Jennifer did say something interesting as to how we can cope with this: the person may not be aware they are exhibiting bad behaviour or using wrong language, but they should not be allowed to do it, being told, as one would tell a child, that this is not acceptable. I would caution that a very gentle style would be needed here. The dementia sufferer will be feeling insecure and frightened, not understanding themselves and not being able to control themselves. We need to see that the person we once knew is still there, however bizarre their language and actions. This would include those who do the strangest things and who even need protecting from themselves. The person may be expressing, as best they can, their fear, anger and their feeling that no one understands them – which is almost certainly true.

For the sufferer, and those suffering with them, this is a journey into the unknown. Stokes writes about a couple where the husband had Alzheimer's and says:

This couple were now to embark upon a journey they had never contemplated to a destination they would never have wished to visit.[22]

Stephanie told me about her husband Alan. They had visited Windsor Castle twice in six months. On the second occasion, they found he had no recollection of the first visit and, from then on, his condition worsened to the point where he now has no language and is in a care home especially designed to cope with advanced dementia. This fine Christian leader kept forgetting things, followed by such a rapid deterioration that he had to be sectioned, despite loving care, distractions and a loving family. Alan grew more distressed, and no medication seemed to work at first. When taken into care, he even attacked the care home staff. Happily, drugs have helped calm him, but he worries and does not know why. Stephanie backs what I wrote earlier: Alan, she says, is still there; it is still 'him'. But this has been a dreadful downhill road, and Stephanie feels in a state of limbo: she is partly a widow, partly responsible for her husband, lacking energy after so much stress.

A couple of miles from Stephanie are Peter and Jennifer, at the beginning of their journey into Peter's recently diagnosed dementia. A brain scan has shown that parts of his brain have died because of Alzheimer's. When the results came through, Jennifer was not surprised, because she had been seeing Peter's memory going. Stephanie, further along the path, told me this is the 'P.A.' level for them, as Jennifer acts as the memory jogger for Peter. These two have determined not to race ahead of the condition and to enjoy their lives as long as they can, believing that God will give them the strength to cope: 'We are in it together with the Lord.' Peter, in his lovely way, told me that he had prayed, 'Thank you for giving me this opportunity.' He seems to be experiencing more of God's love, but Jennifer fears she is losing him already as she seeks to grow closer to God to get her through. 'I gain nothing from worrying now', she said. Theirs will be a tough road.

A key aspect to this journey will be the great need to keep in contact as much as possible. 'The dementia sufferer is trying desperately to maintain contact.'[23] Here, as elsewhere, a balance is needed. Swinton points out that it is presumptuous to know what a dementia sufferer is thinking,[24] but we do need at least to attempt to make a connection as we try to keep in touch, helping the sufferer to converse as best they can. This can be done by being relaxed, making the sufferer feel at ease and always giving them a sense of personal value.

If possible, and accepting what Swinton says, we need to attempt to enter the reality of the person we are now with. This does not mean lying, but in dementia, facts diminish and feelings come to be more important. Trying to have a logical argument will have a great deal less impact than expressing a positive emotion; while we are not reneging on the truths of the Bible, we can still resist the temptation to disagree with odd things which may be said. We are the ones who must go the second mile to be at one with that person who has dementia, which may include letting things go that we do not necessarily agree with. If ever there was a time not to win an argument and lose a friend, this is it.

How are we to cope? I do agree with Carey Mulligan that there needs to be an international effort to combat the disease of dementia, although her assertion that 'dementia is not a natural part of growing old'[25] is not altogether the experience of many. Until progress is made, we have to deal with our present situations, some of us managing better than others. We each need to do it as seems best for ourselves and the dementia sufferer:

> When caring for people with dementia, you cannot
> have inflexible ways of working. People's histories,
> habits and horrors are too complex for this to be so.
> If care is to be truly person centred, it sometimes
> means going against current thinking in order to help
> a person live their life free of torment and foreboding.[26]

When I met with Winifred, I realized how our thinking, current or otherwise, is subject to our emotional state when all goes wrong. Married to Peter, a brilliant Professor of Chemistry, Winifred is an experienced GP, so should, theoretically, have known exactly what to do, having advised many of her own patients and their families about dementia. Did she manage? 'The CT scan showed vascular dementia. I understood, and I fell apart,' she told me. 'I had been trying to say it was old age, but the diagnosis was there and I didn't know how to cope.' Knowing the way things were likely to go was a disadvantage, as Peter, his Christian faith seemingly intact, took that downward path, finally in a care home, where he ultimately refused food and then died quickly.

Winifred was blessed to have a caring family and church fellowship, but it is noteworthy that dementia often carries a stigma. Dementia is seen as a problem, a threat to the world, likely to 'overwhelm health and social services', as the World Health Organisation warned in December 2017.[27] Advice is given that people with dementia should be valued for themselves and not shunned.[28] If we are not careful, we treat older persons as if they were children, speaking to them and about them as such – but they are not children;

they have lifetimes behind them and should be respected for that. I have already made this point, but I emphasize it here as being especially apposite in a case of dementia.

There is a special care needed here, compared with caring for other older people, which is the subject of Chapter 13. I single this out because, with the best will in the world, dementia is a particularly hard condition to be around. It will make a big difference, especially in the earlier stages of dementia, to have people there who love and care. Those known well must be the best, if they have loving hearts. That is what we would all hope for, as John Swinton answered on BBC Radio 4 when asked 'if you ended up having dementia, how would you like to be treated?' He replied, 'I hope that I will be loved and cared for just for who I am, even if who I am is difficult for me and others.'[29] This is an expert writer on the subject, bringing things down to their simplest. That is how we would all want to answer. In similar vein, Tom Kitwood shows the central need in dementia care is love, from which all other needs emanate, such as comfort, identity, attachment and inclusion.[30]

Our wider society can and should play a part in making care a positive experience. The year 2018 began with a heritage industries report saying that tourist sites must become dementia friendly, or they will lose income. It seems that people with dementia spend huge amounts (£11 billion in 2014), and places like the Historic Royal Palaces, including the Tower of London and Hampton Court Palace, should make their sites 'dementia friendly', including having staff with badges saying just that.[31] The Alzheimer's Society has a 'Side by Side' project which matches dementia sufferers with volunteers to keep dementia sufferers active, taking them on trips, keeping up their hobbies and involving them in their local communities. Alas, there are many more people who want help than volunteers, but the scheme is splendid.[32] A garden designer in Edinburgh, Annie Pollock, created a 'forget-me-not' garden with an old fashioned washing line, a bird table and memories to stimulate dementia sufferers.[33]

In very many cases, the best care can only be given, as dementia progresses, in a specialized care home. This is not a surrender or a defeat, but a humble acceptance that both carer and cared for have reached what Oliver James calls the 'tipping point'. This is the moment when the carer says, 'I cannot go on like this' and is best worked out in advance, so good plans are already in place.[34] This is the time when the dementia sufferer will have their well-being best served in a care home or nursing home, probably the latter. As Graham Stokes writes:

> A caring partner doing the best they can in their own home cannot be expected to do everything that is required as a person's dementia unfolds and it is unreasonable for others to make family carers believe this is how it ought to be.[35]

Once this hurdle has been overcome, frequent visits will be massively important, although there must not be a guilt complex about living one's own life as well. We need to leave our own cares behind when visiting, so we can be a blessing and bring a blessing. A smile, a touch or holding of a hand, a lack of questions too hard to answer, and sharing good news will be precious. Bringing flowers, a colourful magazine, a game to play, music to listen to, photos – especially old ones – a favourite Bible passage and a willingness to repeat ad nauseam will make the visit go well. If you arrive with an enthusiastic greeting, go quietly so as not to cause a sad vacuum. The length of the visit does not matter as much as having been there; in later dementia your time will not be remembered, but the warmth will.[36]

In this book, which aims to help us in our faith in later life, the spiritual input during dementia must be primary in our thinking. I therefore return, as promised, to this key area. Once again, I will try to combine personal thoughts with the opinions of those more expert than I. Kitwood gives a helpful starting point: 'Our frame of reference should no longer be person-with-DEMENTIA, but PERSON-with-dementia.'[37] If we look primarily at the disease, we will be clinical; if we look at the sufferer, we will have a better chance of understanding the spiritual context. Dietrich Bonhoeffer, ultimately martyred for his faith in Nazi Germany, makes a triumphant cry as he closes his poem 'Who am I', written while in prison:

> Who am I? They mock me,
> these lonely questions of mine.
> Whoever I am Thou knowest, O God,
> I am Thine![38]

Whatever our condition, we are real people, known by God and – if we are true Christians – belonging to him. Morse speaks of our brains being impaired and asks,

Does that mean that the individual, the person known to God, has changed? Most emphatically it does not.[39]

Roger Hitchings has many years' experience in working with people with dementia. In conversation, he told me that his long-time conclusion is that, even in the most extreme cases, the spiritual life is still operative, although he cannot fully explain how. When major parts of the mind and body fail, there is still a deep, unconscious relationship with God. Dementia does not destroy a person. These are great words from John Wyatt, Professor of Ethics and Perinatology at University College, London:

The Christian view of human nature created in God's image provides a stability of human identity and significance throughout the whole of life, whatever events may befall. Even if my cortex is damaged, or my brain starts to malfunction, or I become confused and disorientated, I will still be me, a unique person, known and loved by others, and ultimately by God himself. No one and nothing can take my human significance from me. I will always be worth what God thinks of me. Even if I become disabled, demented and despised by others, I can retain my own self respect, and I can retain the right to be treated with respect by others.[40]

Wyatt is making a vital point here: we are who we are in God, not in our debilitating human state. When we trust Christ with our lives, we are made new. 'If anyone is in Christ, he is a new creation, the old has gone, the new has come!' (2 Corinthians 5.17). This promise is underlined by Paul's words of assurance in Colossians 3.3: 'For you died, and your life is now hidden with Christ in God.' A person may seem as if their life somehow got lost; we need to rejoice that their life is safely hidden – in Jesus Christ.

> In Christian thought, the dignity of a human being resides, not in what you can do, but in what you are, by creation.[41]

My previous comments, that we are primarily human beings, not human doings, is put much better by these further words from Wyatt. This is why we must believe the magnificent words of Paul:

> I am convinced that neither death nor life, neither angels nor demons, neither the present nor the future, nor any powers, neither height not depth, nor anything else in all creation, will be able to separate us from the love of God that is in Christ Jesus our Lord (Romans 8.38–39).

The all-inclusive sweeping-up phrase 'Nor anything else in all creation' means what it says: dementia, disability, you name it, it is in there. To put this academically, John Swinton says:

> Neurological decline cannot separate us from the love of God and our ongoing vocation as human beings. Lives that are touched by profound forms of dementia have meaning and continuing purpose.[42]

Swinton reiterates that 'nothing can occur to an individual that can make him less of a person,' citing the verses quoted from Romans 8 to prove that.[43] He goes on:

> It is impossible to understand the full meaning of being a human person without first understanding who God is and where human beings stand in relation to God. It is only when we begin to recognize and acknowledge the position of human beings before God that the situation of people with dementia can be fully understood, their personhood authenticated, and their care effectively implemented.[44]

My mother-in-law, Joyce, is 97 and is slowly fading away as her body struggles and her memory lets her down. We chatted about her Christian life. 'It doesn't do anything to affect this: it's with you, part of me, not an outside thing.' Not able to go to church very often, Joyce loves her Bible, 'though I don't understand it all!' Admitting her memory is not good, her words are wise: 'I don't struggle with my faith; I believe completely. I keep this going through sheer belief and sharing it with others who believe. It's part of me.' Here is someone who proves the points made by those I have quoted: Joyce has a true heart relationship with Jesus Christ, not dependent on her condition or her limitations. Her salvation is because nothing can separate her from Christ Jesus. As I have been asked to preach at her funeral, I need to remember this!

A last word on this from Swinton, before moving on to one final area:

Dementia may be a story of great losses, but the fullness of the personhood of sufferers and God's faithful love for them are not among them.[45]

I now turn, in concluding this subject, to the impact this has on both spiritual life and worship. Graham Stokes delightfully writes that 'All people need a reason to get up in the morning,'[46] as he writes about specific dementia sufferers – being a Christian has to be the best reason. How then can we help those who get up with dementia to enjoy their relationship with God? There is much that can be done on a personal basis. An interesting article appeared in *Evangelical Times* in 2010 by the Australian Peter Barnes, about reaching people with dementia, intellectual disabilities and brain damage.[47] He begins by citing the Westminster Confession, which states that infants who die, plus those 'who are incapable of being outwardly called by the ministry of the Word' are not excluded from salvation. He then makes some practical suggestions as to how we can help these sufferers, beginning with the need for us to believe that God loves them, which will impact our whole approach.

Barnes believes that the Bible's words can be effective in reaching into a person's inner being and gives examples from his experience where this has clearly touched those with dementia. I would couple this with prayer, which is able to awaken the spiritual life more than anything. Billy Graham writes movingly of a visit he made to former President Reagan (with whom we started this chapter) in his later stages of dementia. Graham felt Reagan had not recognized him and any conversation was one-sided.

Nancy Reagan asked Graham to pray as he always had when Reagan was President. As Mrs Reagan walked to the car with him, Graham asked her if her husband had recognized him, to which she replied, 'Not until you prayed – but hearing you then, I believe he knew who was praying for him.'[48]

It was the prayer which got through, as it seems to do when nothing else works. Ken, a former national evangelist, lived until his death in Easter week, 2018, in a nursing home, with increasing dementia; in response to friends chatting with him, he merely mumbled and grunted in reply at best. His growing dementia was distressing to the close friends who visited him, but they resolved to be positive and, in particular, always share a brief passage from the Bible and pray with him. A close friend of mine, John, was very faithful in this and told me how, soon before Ken's death, he read Psalm 42 to Ken and then prayed, whereupon Ken added his 'Amen', the only distinct word of the entire visit. This, John says, is what happened most times, as the 'spiritual' part of the visit impacted Ken as nothing else seemed to. I believe it is no coincidence that John read Psalm 42. Verse seven says that 'Deep calls to deep', with Biblical scholars using this to show how God gets through to our inmost spirits, whatever appears to be happening on the surface. God does speak to the 'deep' parts of our lives, whatever our condition. I would echo this from my own family. My stepmother, Ethel, was a wonderful teacher, full of knowledge and joy, until several strokes meant that she ended up unable to finish many a sentence. However, as she slowly deteriorated, two things happened. The first was that she became more generous in her love and praise for her family. Second, my father related an amazing thing: each night, as they lay in bed, he would suggest that they prayed before they slept. Until that moment, Ethel had been unable to communicate in a meaningful way. Yet, after my father had prayed, she would then pray the most wonderful, deeply spiritual prayers, with no hint of hesitation or confusion. My father said they were much deeper in meaning than anything she prayed before the strokes began. They would then say the Lord's Prayer and the 'Grace', again without hesitation, after which she returned to her forgetfulness.

I believe it is possible to begin to explain what was happening there if we take seriously the words of Paul in Romans:

> You received the Spirit of sonship. And by him we cry, 'Abba, Father'. The Spirit himself testifies with our spirit that we are God's children. Now if we are children, then we are heirs - heirs of God and co-heirs with Christ, if indeed we share in his sufferings in order that we may also share his glory (Romans 8.15–17).

For a Christian with dementia, this 'witness', as Roger Hitchings has pointed out to me, 'goes beyond mere intellectual activity and is a direct witness by the Holy Spirit to the spirit of a believer.' Roger directed me to the way the Holy Spirit worked in Elizabeth, when her unborn child (later John the Baptist) recognized the unborn Jesus and leapt in her womb (Luke 1.39–45). Roger equates this with the Holy Spirit working in the inner being of a believer with dementia, even though the intellectual capacities may be impaired. He said this in writing to me:

> The reality of ongoing spiritual life is seen in the effective influence of the word read, truth sung and prayer taking place where rementing occurs.

This would certainly explain my stepmother's reaction to her times of prayer with my father and is replicated by the testimony of others who have been involved with people like her. We need to flag this up in our continuing writings on this subject, speaking of the spirituality of those with dementia.

To take the Barnes article further, he next speaks of 'means of grace', mentioning specifically the Lord's Supper, which, he says, is sometimes a very effective means of reaching a dementia-suffering Christian with their memories of previous services. The physical touch of bread and wine enables a real 'communion' in body and heart (1 Cor. 10.16, where Paul says the cup/bread is communion with the blood/body of Christ). If possible, this can be in the context of a church service or a fellowship at home, but it is good one-to-one as well. Perhaps more than any other form of service, this will be part of a remembered history. To this can be added Barnes' assertion that 'Christian songs can minister in a way we cannot.' For my 65th birthday, my very musical son Andy recorded a personal CD of my favourite choruses and hymns, for when I get dementia! I do listen to them now, of course.

Dr Jennifer Bute shared with me a lovely story of her visiting a friend with dementia, who came out with the incongruous line, 'Saturday. Peas are green on Saturday.' This was repeated several times, with Jennifer trying such diversionary tactics as 'So is grass.' 'Yes – but peas . . .' On and on it went until Jennifer started to sing, 'Yesterday, today, forever, Jesus is the same.' To her relief, her friend remembered the old chorus, joined in – and the peas were forgotten! There is no doubt how profound an impact Christian music does have, individually and in group worship. I would want to emphasize the key role worship can have in the life of dementia sufferers.

> Religious people need to worship God. People with dementia who have a faith have the same need.[49]

When I go to parts of East Africa, I see a remarkable tree, the baobab. I have seen these trees in the rainy season, with their beautiful vividly green leaves and fruit like small coconuts. It is sometimes called 'the tree of life'. But when the rains go, and the long dry season sets in, the baobab slowly retreats into itself, until all the leaves are gone, the fruit has fallen and the tree appears to be completely dead. The huge trunk just stands there, as if it were ready to fall over. But, deep inside, it is hugging its life, ready for the rains. It is a beautiful reminder of all who, in their hidden-away dementia, are awaiting the new life Jesus will bring when he calls them to his home or when he returns in glory. The life is there. Let's not chop the tree down; there is life and beauty deep inside.

13

Who cares?

Question: Who cares? Answer: Most of us. Dementia is a big challenge, but only 11 per cent of care is in this area. Here are some statistics which amaze me:

There are seven million carers at any one time in the UK, one in ten of the population, and rising.

One in five of everyone aged 50 to 64 is a carer.

One in four carers is a mental health carer.

Nearly one in eight people in employment also are carers.

Three in every five will be a carer at some stage of their lives.

Out of 800,000 with dementia, 670,000 have unpaid carers, two thirds being spouses.

The bad news is that 53 per cent of carers have to borrow money to care, with over 68 per cent of older carers saying that being a carer has an adverse affect on their mental health.

Here is the most mind-blowing statistic of all: carers save the national economy £132 billion each year.

These figures, from the Carer's Trust,[1] show that we are all in this, either personally or by being very close to a carer. Henri Nouwen, looking at our early lives as well as our later days, comments that 'Life is lived from dependence to dependence.'[2] This care is either at home or 'in care', involves both cared for and carer and, very importantly, must have a major Christian element to it. We shall take each point in turn.

Caring at home

How do we view the idea of caring for another? Billy Graham writes of his father-in-law, Dr Nelson Bell, a former missionary in China, caring for his wife Virginia after she suffered a series of strokes, refusing to move her into a nursing home. Someone asked him about this decision, to which he replied, 'This is my calling now.'[3] Smiling at each other on our wedding day, 'In sickness and in health' implied the latter, but the former comes along. Nouwen was right, we are cared for as we start our lives, then we care, then we are cared for. In this world of independence, where we each 'do our own thing', here is a call back to reality from one of our eminent medical specialists John Wyatt:

> God has not made us as independent individuals sprouting up like mushrooms in a field. He has put us in families, linked together in mutual dependence. Not only are we designed to depend on God: we are designed to depend on one another.[4]

The challenge of Paul rings down the years: 'Carry each other's burdens, and in this way you will fulfil the law of Christ' (Galatians 6.2). To carry a burden is a hard thing, to carry another's burden means sharing their pain; it is costly and challenging. It involves seeing the intrinsic value in each and every person, regardless of their condition and situation. Paul puts it very strongly:

> Those parts of the body that seem to be weaker are indispensable, and the parts that we think are less honourable we treat with special honour . . . so that there should be no division in the body, but that its parts should have equal concern for each other. If one part suffers, every part suffers with it; if one part is honoured, every part rejoices with it (1 Corinthians 12.22–26).

Reverting back to Galatians 6, Paul sees this caring in the context of how we should live our whole lives in this way:

> As we have opportunity, let us do good to all people, especially to those who belong to the family of believers (Galatians 6.10).

As with many of the Bible's injunctions, it is a great theory which, as will be shown, is not always followed in practice. In essence, it means being there, wherever the need of a person is reachable. We cannot carry the burdens of the whole world, but we should not be crossing over the road to avoid the needy as we pass by, as the story of the good Samaritan taught (Luke 10.25–37). I know of friends who have literally had church folk cross the street to avoid them so as not to have to ask about a hardship.[5] Conversely, many others do see the needs of others as an opportunity to follow the two sets of verses above and to care as they should. So often we wonder, in our later years, if we can be of any use at all: here is a God-given opportunity. We do want to serve God; being allowed to care for others is a wonderful way of being obedient as well as being useful.

A couple of key points need to be made at this juncture, the first being that carers are of all ages and care for all ages, so, although this book is primarily about us older ones, nevertheless this chapter can be interpreted for anyone to whom 'caring' applies. Second, I recognize that we Christians have no exclusivity to being those who care; indeed, many who seem to have no faith at all often put us to shame. *The Times* Magazine carried extracts from a new book by Greg Wise about his care for his terminally ill sister Clare, showing his devotion to her as she came towards her death. He spoke of how a friend who is a vicar gave him good advice: the person with the need can throw you all their problems, which you can then throw further outwards. Conversely, the problems on the outside, and yours, must not be thrown inwards. His love and care for his sister comes through with a real passion and challenges those of us with faith to emulate such love.[6]

My sister-in-law Judy, with her husband Richard, has four generations for whom they care: 'So I'm always caring,' says Judy. In her sixties, still working three days a week, she has her 97-year-old mother living with her, giving up their living room to accommodate her. Richard admits that Judy looks after him, and an adult daughter still lives at home – and the other four children look to Judy for help, especially those with children, whom Judy looks after frequently. Her situation will be mirrored in lots of families. Many a time Judy has to drop everything for one or another. 'It's part of life,' she says. Speaking of her mother, Judy admits that her life is restricted by being the main carer, but 'it is my duty and privilege to look after her'; she is glad of two sisters who share some of the care and grateful for friends who visit. But it is hard. She is often unable to go out in the evening, it is a struggle to arrange holidays, and it is exhausting when her mother is ill.

I tell Judy's story because the challenges from St Paul face people like Judy who have to work them out in practical terms. Knowing my mother-in-law well, I know how enormously grateful she is. Speaking with others like her, this care is vital. I will refer to 'Susan' later, but her mother, who lives alone, but near enough to Susan for her to see her every day, told me how crucial this close-by care is. 'When my husband died, Susan, living close by, became my carer, doing everything possible to make my life easier. She never becomes so poorly that she has to miss her visits to me.' Carers like Judy and Susan are essential for these very elderly parents to survive at home. How long these carers can cope will depend on differing factors: the declining health of both cared-for and carer, the support available, the age of both parties, to mention only a few. Stephanie, mentioned in the last chapter, whose husband deteriorated with dementia, sought all the professional help she could, but in the end, Social Services told her that Alan had to go into care: Stephanie was not getting any sleep, Alan was being hostile and his behaviour was beyond her strength. So many struggle on to their own detriment.

Care at home is almost exclusively done by family members for family members. The great strength here is that we know each other well. Visitors are splendid for conversations and for bringing news and gossip. More important still, as Morse and Hitchings tell us:

> The key to really good, person-centred care is communication. Communication is much more than talking and listening, important though they are. Sitting silently alongside someone, just holding their hand. . . . says a lot to a lonely person.[7]

When I visited my father, I would often find him doing just that, as he and my stepmother held hands as they sat next to each other, conversation nonexistent and yet at peace, despite her several debilitating strokes. I know an elderly couple where the wife, caring for her husband as he slowly lost his sight, had almost telepathic communication skills.[8]

When considering this subject of caregiving, we must not forget the care given by older people for the young. A strong letter written by Ann Buchanan, Emeritus professor of social work at the University of Oxford, which made the lead in *The Times*' 'Letters to the Editor' in November 2017, included this:

> Grandparents today play a significant role in providing childcare and many children develop strong relationships with their grandparents, not only in the early years but through adolescence . . . Research has shown that young people look upon their grandparents as a safety net.

Buchanan urges that, in divorce cases, there should be orders for ongoing contact between children and grandparents, in the interests of those children.[9] The organization Grandparents Plus has reported, also in November 2017, that some 200,000 children in the United Kingdom are raised by a family member other than a parent, with the burden falling on grandparents, many of whom fall into huge debts as a result. Cheryl Ward, for the charity Family Fund said:

> There is a longstanding issue with support for grandparent carers: they are not recognised financially, as someone with special guardianship is.[10]

Although these references indicate problems, the truth is that, whatever the cost, we grandparents love this sort of care. My friend Gail put it this way: 'Being a carer is a commitment – but a wonderful one.' Gail has a life in the North East of England, but frequently goes for two or three weeks at a time to care for grandchildren, so that busy parents can go out to work. The main problem is being in charge and yet not being in authority; the rules of the home have to be followed, even if they would not have been your rules if you had been the parent. The long journeys down South, the times away from home and friends: 'I love it! I love my small grandchildren.' Gail's words are those of many a grandparent, as the older generation cares for the next-but-one generation.

Some of this chapter could have been included in the earlier section where I considered what older people can do. This is a fair point, but inevitably there will be an occasional overlap. What I am seeking to do here is deal specifically with care. Grandparents, as I have explained, find themselves in this four-way caring situation: for their own parents, for their contemporaries, for their children and, finally, their grandchildren. It is a great challenge.

The wider family can and does help. What about the wider church family, to pick up again the words of Paul in 1 Corinthians 12? If we want Christian people to be 'old and faithful', to have 'faith in later years', as this book's title urges, then the body of Christ must have a key role to play when considering care at home. John Wyatt draws attention to James 1.27, which speaks of true religion, acceptable to God, being 'to look after orphans and widows in their distress', asking what is the modern equivalent of these. In a long list, he includes 'the brain damaged adult, the elderly sufferer with Alzheimer's disease and the psychiatric patient.'[11] To those I would want to add the housebound and their carers. Rob Merchant had something very strong to say to me when we chatted about the subject: 'The church dismembers by not visiting, not caring, not helping the wife with her weekly shop.' He believes, and I agree wholeheartedly, that church leaders need to model this caring for the modern equivalents of 'the orphan and the widow.' There should be visiting – and sitting praying with those who are cared for is part of the expectation of God for ministers. Merchant says that not to visit is, in his word, 'rotten'. He dares to take this even further: ministers have the gift of time and, if they do not offer that gift or do not see the need to exercise that gift, they should not have got ordained. Strong words indeed, but right. Richard Ford says this:

> Visiting the sick is really a priest's line of work, not an
> ex-realtor's. Priests have something to bring – ceremony,
> forgetfulness, a few stale, vaguely off-colour jokes leading
> to forgiveness. I only have an orthopaedic pillow.[12]

I may not agree with all the former American estate agent
Richard Ford writes, but I agree with his sentiments. Ignore
the rude jokes, but there is the ceremony of a home communion and the blessing of forgiveness. So much can be done
by the church family, leaders and members alike. Louise
Morse and Roger Hitchings write specifically about dementia, but their advice works for all who are cared for at home.
They rightly say that the secret is a lot of organization, so
the work is shared. The idea is to get a group together who
are willing to be involved, saying that 'support and encouragement cannot come from one individual on their own.'
This is probably true, but should not put off a lone Christian
who is willing to do what others cannot or will not. These
writers go on to urge that the group finds out from the carer
some background on the person to be visited and what will
help most. Especially with dementia, there needs to be both
sensitivity and understanding. Could the church members
help to give lifts to church, have a special 'club' maybe for a
weekly lunch or, if the person is housebound, pray for them
in the service?[13] We are meant to be a team; let's play like
one.

There is one final area here which is of very special significance, emphasized by Henri Nouwen, whose book *Our
Greatest Gift* is about caring for the dying. Here are two
quotations from this:

To care for others as they become weaker and closer to death is to allow them to fulfil their deepest vocation, that of becoming ever more fully what they already are: daughters and sons of God.

Caring for the dying means helping the dying discover that, in their increasing weakness, God's strength becomes visible.

He makes a plea for dignity in dying, but, even more, that we enable those who are dying to find a deep fulfilment at this last stage of their life here on earth. With his years of experience, living as he did in a community which cared for many who were terminally ill, these are challenging words. It is remarkable to see in his words how the process of dying can be a blessing, showing in a new way the relationship we have with God as our Father. As our strength ebbs, so we are able to rely on and feel the power of God in a special way. Nouwen goes on to challenge a negative approach: 'In running away from the dying, we bury our precious gift of care.'[14] His words call for a positive attitude and response.

No more needs to be said.

Caring 'in care'

Here, where men sit and hear each other groan;
Where palsy shakes a few, sad, last grey hairs.[15]

I doubt if Keats had care homes and nursing homes in mind when he penned these lines in his incomparable 'Ode to a Nightingale', but in some places I visit, it does feel a bit like this. When we have to choose a place for care outside our own home, whether for ourselves or for a loved one, we need to find a good one. At present, some 20 per cent of those over 65 die in a care home,[16] so this choice affects many of us. Rather in the same way as we put off writing a will, so the matter of where we might reside if and when we need residential care is a 'back burner' discussion for a later date. If we want a genuinely Christian care or nursing home, they are not to be found in great quantities. We should, at least, be looking for somewhere which will be user-friendly and sympathetic to an ageing and ailing Christian.

> All human beings have a need to belong, to be recognised and to be accepted. Care homes are little communities, and individuals need to know they are a valued part of it.[17]

This advice from Morse and Hitchings is often easier said than done, with many homes now run by agencies, having staff from around the world, for some of whom even the English language itself is a challenge. There are all sorts of 'ginger' groups attempting to improve things. Some care homes encourage children's nurseries to share their life, giving a happy inter-generational relationship.[18] Others are encouraging schools and care homes to be built near each other to give age groups the chance to mingle.[19] I do like these ideas. There is a great danger of care homes and nursing homes being exclusively for the very old and ill, where the only people who are there are in these categories, except younger members of staff. The whole concept of 'family' is lost.

Looking into the future, another style of care home specifically for dementia sufferers may bring a completely different approach, with the construction of 'dementia villages', based on the groundbreaking Dutch village at Hogeweyk. Here, dementia sufferers live in small groups, based on their backgrounds and interests, which include 'upper class', 'homely', 'cultural' and, interestingly, one labelled 'Christian'. Plans are afoot for such a site in Kent, with another proposed for Scotland. Villages like Hogeweyk are springing up in Australia, America and Germany and are said to be hugely better than other care homes, giving opportunities for sufferers to enjoy life more and to help each other.[20] At present, it is a case of 'wait and see'.

In the meantime, we need to understand that we have a job to do, because our visits to those in care homes become a lifeline, a link with the outside world and a link with the human family and the church family, if only for the length of the time together. If it is mealtime and we are part of the family of the person being visited, the old 'grace' we used to say at those long ago mealtimes is the one to pray; the same sort of banter we shared around the table can be a part of the conversation, the old expressions recalled. My stepmother used the lovely phrase 'down red lane' when encouraging a child to eat – what a joy to use that with her if she needed feeding. It goes without saying that this was in no way treating her like a child, but helping her in a fun way when she could not feed herself and enjoying the joking reference to her own former style. The comment, as well as the food, always went down well! If the person has their own room, as they usually do, can we help in a practical way, asking first if it is alright to dust or tidy or put things where they would be most appreciated and easily seen? Chats need to be positive, and it is often good to be reactive. As older people's minds struggle with reality, we may have to enter their alternative world. It is not lying when we agree that their Mum will be popping round: what is the point of saying that she is long dead? Happy tales of life outside the home will light up the day. I would never want to leave without a prayer, a simple heartfelt one – more of that shortly.

We who visit (or who should visit) those in care have a duty to rescue bad situations. The Scottish edition of The Times on 6 February 2018 carried a sad article headed 'Terminally ill "not cared for properly",' saying that 'One in four Scots believes a relative or close friend with terminal illness did not get the care they needed.' It included a comment from Susan Lowes, Marie Curie policy and publicity affairs manager in Scotland: 'We continue to hear that terminally ill people don't get the care they need – or it comes too late.'[21] If this be true, then care organizations should be making waves to change things, as should anyone who sees bad practice.

Dr Ranjana Srivastava wrote a moving article in *The Guardian* in October 2017 on the loneliness and lostness of some of his elderly patients in hospital, saying how he, as a doctor, could not 'replace the strongest medicine of all: attentive kindness to stave off loneliness.' He went on:

I sit down at a desk, reflecting on an entire weekend of taking histories, postulating diagnoses and prescribing drugs when all the while, the greatest enemy has been the loneliness of patients, who feel ignored, neglected, or outright abandoned by their family. I count that during the entire weekend we met only a handful of adult relatives and not a single child.[22]

This is heart-breaking, but not hopeless. Those of us who are Christians can do something, especially in the area of sharing spiritually.

Worship

To use a heading with the single word 'Worship' needs clarification, or it could mislead. The older I get, the more I realize that our whole lives are worship. Paul's famous words are such a challenge: 'I urge you . . . in view of God's mercy, to offer your bodies as living sacrifices, holy and pleasing to God – this is your spiritual act of worship' (Romans 12.1). In personal relationships, the words we often claim in church are particularly appropriate for one-to-one encounters: 'Where two or three come together in my name, there am I with them' (Matthew 18.20). I pick up my promise to mention prayer. I am utterly convinced, not only of the efficacy of prayer, but of the value of praying. I want to encourage personal prayer when with someone being visited, at home or in a care/nursing home. I often use the excuse of an ageing 'forgettery', so that if someone asks me, 'Will you pray for me / someone else / a situation?' I respond by telling them how quickly I forget and inviting them to pray with me right then. I have never been refused; on the contrary, this immediate prayer has been much valued, and the person has been left glad that they heard my prayer.

This works at a distance. At a nearby church, we used to have, before she went into a nursing home, an elderly organist. She and I always chatted about the hymns for any service I was leading. Grace was a quiet lady, sometimes unsure of her faith, with a great gift for finding hymns which dovetailed with the theme of the service. At the end of one telephone conversation, I said, almost without thinking, 'Bless you, Grace!' Her response surprised me: 'Oh, thank you! A personal blessing!' She meant it, and it changed my whole attitude to off-the-cuff remarks: to 'bless' someone is to pray for them, as Grace knew. I would very rarely leave a visit without a real 'blessing' in a prayer, often holding the person's hand or putting my hand on their shoulder. It has such value, as the person prayed for knows that you have indeed prayed. We show we care so deeply that we bring God into that care. 'May I pray before I go?' in my experience never gets 'No' for a response.

When there are more than one visiting, a small act of worship may be the only opportunity for a 'live' service the cared-for is able to have, compared with one from the radio or TV. Even one-to-one, there can be a reading from the Bible as well as prayer, possibly a favourite hymn or chorus. But with a group in a care home, or more than three or four at home, there is no reason why a simple service cannot be conducted, probably very informally. If your church does not visit the care homes nearby, this is a real shame. Most homes, if approached in a sensitive way, are glad to let their residents have an occasional opportunity to worship and, in my experience, will enable this to happen in one of their lounges. London City Mission, for example, encourages monthly teams to have services which include hymns, a Scripture reading, prayer and a simple talk. Large-print words, a keyboard and some refreshments will all help, as will a few good singers.[23]

I do not know of a better way of doing this than that organized in Lindfield, Sussex, by a team including Peter and Keith, already mentioned in the chapters about dementia (Peter) and coping with the death of a partner (Keith). These two men, with their wives Jennifer and Olive, felt God's call to share God's love with the seven care and nursing homes in their small town in Sussex. They began in the care home where they were the house managers, where they saw the benefit of a regular Sunday service, and prayer with several individuals. None of the other care and nursing homes seemed to have any church involvement, so Peter was asked to head up a team who could go to each home with the offer of services and spiritual care. Every head of every home agreed. They offered a monthly service with a simple Communion or a 'service of the Word', plus friendship, support and visiting. In one home, the service became weekly; in another, fortnightly.

The whole thing snowballed. Between a half and three quarters of the residents would join the services, as staff and volunteers enabled residents to get to the room. Christians grew in their faith, non-churchgoers came to faith, a 'Senior Alpha' course was run on many occasions and sick or dying residents were visited individually. Two further ventures also took off: Peter found that several families asked whether he would conduct the funeral service of a resident, because he had been a help and a blessing and had been trusted. Both Peter and Keith decided that when a resident died, they would hold a short and simple bedside service to say farewell, which the staff really appreciated. Peter, with his heart for reaching people for Jesus, saw many come to faith.

One final thing needs to be underlined: a considerable number of the residents were in various stages of dementia, but this did not affect what happened. Often the dementia sufferer would open up more in the service than at any other time, joining in a well-known hymn, remembered from long ago, with great happiness. Worship is a great leveller, and all can be blessed. Of course there should never be the slightest coercion, and a gracious style is the way to do it. We Christians have a special opportunity here.

Care for the carers

We shouldn't try to care by ourselves. Care is not an endurance test. We should, whenever possible, care together with others. It is the community of care that reminds the dying person of his or her belovedness.[24]

If you go it alone and expect to provide 24 hour wrap-around care singlehandedly for the rest of the client's life, you will go bonkers or suffer a physical collapse.[25]

These two observations from Nouwen and James, writing respectively about near-death and dementia care, say one very important thing: caring is a tough calling, and the carer should not be in there alone. 'Who cares for the carer?' is a question often asked but less often answered satisfactorily. Oliver James goes on to make two further points. The first is that even the experts appreciate help:

> Most professionals are only too happy for help with cases of dementia, being all too often overstretched and eager for any assistance going.[26]

If that be true for those whose job it is to care, how much more for the vast numbers who care at home, who need relief. James then says what is obvious but needs stating, which is that the carer needs an activity other than caring, something pleasurable, to get them away from their single role as a carer. He points out something which may not be so obvious: when the time comes for the cared-for to move into a care home, the carer having other interests already in place will not leave a vacuum of 'What am I going to do now?'[27]

Tom Kitwood picks up James' point about those employed in care homes and nursing homes, saying how vital it is to care for them. Do they have good pay and conditions of service? Are they taught how to do their job, both when they start and with ongoing in-service training? Are they properly supervised as part of a team? Are they really the right people for the job? Do they have adequate time away from their work, especially if they live onsite?[28] Kitwood's book *Dementia Reconsidered* carries the subtitle *The Person Comes First*, and it is appropriate, with this in mind, to consider the carer's needs, so they are not simply a person who works, but a human being with a life to live.

So far, everything seems clear. Carers need help, which does not require a degree in social sciences to enable it to be given. Most people are able to do a bit of housecleaning, get some shopping, sit and chat for a while with the cared-for or the carer, or both. We can all hold a conversation, make a cup of tea or coffee and be there while the carer goes off for a couple of hours. Many churches and communities have meetings and groups for older people: a lift for a housebound person will relieve the carer and give them some more free time. Perhaps most of all, for those of us who are Christians, we can share those things which will stimulate faith, for both carer and cared-for: a prayer, an opening of the Bible or a good Christian book. The carer's needs are very straightforward in most cases, and with a little effort and imagination, those needs can be met by most of us.

Why is it, then, when I read what the experts say or talk with carers, that things do not happen like this? We are not being asked to work miracles, unless the miracle is that we are there.

> Suffering in another human being is a call to the rest of us to stand in community. It is a call to be there. Suffering is not a question which demands an answer, it is not a problem which requires a solution, it is a mystery which demands a presence.[29]

Wyatt has it right. So why does Morse have to say that it is not unusual for people with dementia and their families to feel 'abandoned'?[30] That is a strong word to use. Wyatt agrees, saying that 'It is easy for carers to feel isolated, ignored and demeaned.'[31] For an expert doctor, these are emotive words. Because of all this, Morse and Hitchings say of carers:

It is not surprising that they invariably suffer from stress, chronic fatigue, anger, guilt and depression. These symptoms are increasingly being referred to as 'caregiver syndrome' by the medical community. Dr Jean Posner, a neuropsychiatrist in Baltimore, Maryland, calls caregiver syndrome 'a debilitating condition brought on by unrelieved, constant caring for a person with a chronic illness or dementia'.[32]

A close friend in the South of England talked with me and exhibited some of these symptoms. She spoke of caring for her mother and being 'at the end of my tether, verging on a breakdown, in tears at the doctor's surgery.' With her mother living a few doors away, in her nineties, my friend – in her sixties – has to look after two homes, with all the cleaning, gardening, shopping, cooking and taking her mother to appointments. 'I struggle with intrusive questioning and criticism, because I'm the only one around to give any interest in life or to get stroppy with! I struggle with not being able to see my daughter and grandchildren very often, because I'm tied to looking after Mum.' And yet – and here is the rub – 'I wouldn't not do it, and I know, despite the difficulties, this is a God-given opportunity to care for Mum.'

My friend says that this is the secret of being able to carry on. 'Once I accepted this is God's will for me at the moment,

I stopped feeling angry and stopped feeling I didn't matter. We only make our own situation worse by trying to fight it. I was trying to carve out a life of my own, when God wanted me to give up my life. When I agreed to give up my life, the blessings started to flow.' She quoted to me Haggai 2.19, where, when we give our best to God, 'From this day on I will bless you.'

I am left amazed by this friend of mine. Here is the very tough secret of care: if no one else is around, we have to submit ourselves to the will of God and find, in so doing, that we are blessed. So often, there is no one else. My neighbour Christine, a retired minister, now cares for her elderly husband; she tells me she has no family to help, nobody to share. She feels dragged down, as her own old age means that she tires as she gets her husband up, showered, dressed, breakfasted – exhausting her. However, Christine is working out that there is help and she can be cared for. First, God is there. Christine finds contemplative prayer works wonderfully, as do Christian friends who visit. She takes advantage of respite care in a nearby town for her husband, a week at a time working best. Books on spirituality also help. Having been a minister has plus and minus results. Negatively, people feel a little reluctant to help. Positively, Christine now acts as a spiritual director to nine or ten people, who come to her home, giving her a real purpose, as well as friendship and companionship. Despite someone telling her that, with having to care for her husband, 'It's clipped your wings a bit!' (people can say cruel things), Christine has worked out how she can be cared for. How essential this is for every carer.

Each carer will be in a unique situation, so solutions will vary. Are there people in the church, the neighbourhood or the family, who will come on a regular basis to sit and chat, giving the carer time to escape for a while? Is there a church or community coffee morning? There are professional helpers who can be there in the morning and evening. The key is not to go it alone. I find that, living a long way from many of my friends, a phone call to encourage is much appreciated. Simple acts of kindness are valued. Christine's use of respite care needs to be taken up as a great way for a break. All of us can make the resolve to do something to help. John Piper quotes Jonathan Edwards:

> In some sense the most benevolent, generous person in the world seeks his own happiness in doing good to others, because he places his happiness in their good. His mind is so enlarged as to take them, as it were, into himself.[33]

Individuals and churches need to hear these words. Despite the negative comments I hear about churches not caring for carers, I was heartened by the positive experience of Keith, whom we have met earlier and who cared for his wife Olive. He saw his caring as an opportunity to give back to the wife who had always cared for him. He told me how God provided for him through 'his servants', who brought meals, prayed and visited. We need to let people help, as Keith did.

I close this chapter with a quotation I used in my book on bereavement, which seems apposite here:

It was Augustine who said, 'I have read in Plato and Cicero sayings that are wise and very beautiful; but I never read in either of them, "Come to me, all you who are weary and burdened, and I will give you rest."' Such are the words of Jesus in Matthew 11:28.[34]

If you are a carer, may they bless you.

14

Go for it!

When all is said and done, there is often much more said than done. Aesop said that a long time ago.[1] A lot has been said in this book; will we do anything about it? I have two soccer stories to sandwich some words of encouragement.

Manchester United is a very good football team. I say this through gritted teeth, being a fan of Leeds United, who struggle by comparison. Of all Manchester United's managers, many would hold up Sir Matt Busby as the best. In the 1950s, he had a team famously known as 'The Busby Babes', whose football was magnificent. On 6 February 1958, flying home from a European match, the plane carrying the team crashed at Munich, killing the majority of the team and badly injuring Busby. Instead of giving up, Busby recovered, rebuilt a new team and, ten years later, won the European Cup.

What was the secret of Matt Busby's managerial skills? Other United managers have been known for their abilities of shouting, kicking football boots at players, or scowling and pointing. Not Busby; he had a different approach. As the players rose in the dressing room to go out and win again, Busby said these words in his quiet, positive way: 'Do it simply. Do it well. Do it now.'

In the mid 1980s, I was encouraged to found the 40.3 Trust (after Psalm 40.3) and was joined at its inception by a fine young man as Trust Manager – Mark Jarvis. His expertise was crucial, and after some years, he moved to greater things, including writing (with Chris Powell) a splendid book on team building, *Uncle Bob Builds a Boat*.[2] When he left, he gave me a Bible, which is now well-used, well-worn and, currently, has given all the Scripture quotations in this book. He wrote this in the front:

> Ian. With apologies to Sir Matt Busby: 'They need it simple, they need it presented well and they need it NOW!' As God's man for our generation, be sure I am praying for you every time you give it to them. Mark

I neither deserved his generosity nor his kind belief in me, but I have sought to follow his advice in my ministry and writing. It is my belief that this is how we can succeed in living our Christian lives in our later years, by sticking to a simple style, by doing it well and doing it now. Do you feel optimistic or pessimistic about these latter years? Here are a couple of final thoughts, for whichever is your approach. Let's be optimistic first.

St Paul had a tough life. He spoke on more than one occasion of facing his impending death, yet exuded an optimism which could be ours. He writes about this in 2 Corinthians 4.6–18. As we get older, we need to come back to basics, like Matt Busby did. Our basic faith is not in an ability to play a game, but to live a life centred on our perfect 'manager', Jesus:

> For God, who said 'Let light shine out of darkness', made his light shine in our hearts to give us the light of

the knowledge of the glory of God in the face of Christ
(v 6).

Here is Paul's optimism: he looks to Jesus for his light and
for the glory of Jesus to be in his life. In the midst of his
sufferings, Paul looks on the face of Jesus. I used to sing as
a teenager:

> Turn your eyes upon Jesus,
> Look full in his wonderful face.[3]

I remembered those words when our little home group
recently studied Revelation, where John describes Jesus in
his glory: 'His face was like the sun shining in all its bril-
liance' (Revelation 1.16). From what both Paul and John say,
whatever life holds in my later years, I know I can face it
with him. When the going gets hard, the words of another
old song echo in my mind:

> By and by when I look on his face,
> Beautiful face, thorn-shadowed face.
> By and by when I look on his face,
> I'll wish I had given him more.[4]

These later years of our lives need to be lived in the light
of Jesus, 'the true light that gives light to every man'
(John 1.9). Of course, there are seriously hard times, but
this light of Jesus is different: 'The light shines in the
darkness' (John 1.4). Here is the source of our optimism.
Optimists are allowed to have a degree of realism, and I

accept Paul's caution that 'we have this treasure in jars of clay' (v 7), probably a bit cracked here and there and, in all probability, leaking. I love the story of the old lady who said she needed the Holy Spirit to keep filling her every day and when asked why, replied, 'Because I leak!' With our old pottery, we are still clay in the potter's hand (Jeremiah 18.1–6), and he keeps re-shaping and re-making us. If we say we are 'hard pressed, perplexed, struck down, given over to death,' we are quoting selectively. Paul agreed these things are true and then adds the little word 'but' to give an answer in this way:

> We are hard pressed on every side, BUT not
>   crushed;
> Perplexed, BUT not in despair;
> Persecuted, BUT not abandoned;
> Struck down, BUT not destroyed.
> (vs 8, 9)

I have taken the liberty of putting capitals where Paul does not, to emphasize the point. When Paul says that 'death is at work in us' (v 12), he does so to show that the life of Jesus 'may be revealed in our mortal body' (v 10). In these few verses in 2 Corinthians 4, the dying Paul oozes positivity. We are not waiting for the coming glory to be made new; Jesus is in our ageing 'mortal bodies' right now. This is one of the great New Testament passages where we are said to have God's glory in the here and now. Paul re-emphasizes again in this Chapter 4 what he has told his readers in the previous chapter:

> We, who with unveiled faces all reflect the Lord's glory, are being transformed into his likeness with ever-increasing glory, which comes from the Lord, who is the Spirit (2 Corinthians 3.18).

We are new; we are special; we have God's glory in us today. We can and must let this flow in us and through us, enabling us to make a difference for good.

If you think you are too old to be of any use now, remember the African proverb: 'If you think you are too small to make a difference, try sleeping in a closed room with a mosquito.' God's mercies are 'New every morning' (Lamentations 3.23), which is the best reason for rising to meet each new day. Getting old? For sure! Now hear this:

> We do not lose heart. Though outwardly we are wasting away, yet inwardly we are being renewed day by day. For our light and momentary troubles are achieving for us an eternal glory that far outweighs them all. So we fix our eyes not one what is seen, but on what is unseen. For what is seen is temporary, but what is unseen is eternal (2 Corinthians 4.16–18).

Our risen and ascended Saviour, the Lord Jesus Christ, has given us what some call 'a glimpse around the corner of the tapestry being woven.' See you there!

Here is another soccer story, which is my favourite and gives the title to this chapter. Sunday, 17 May 1987 was a day like no other. As a family we went to church in the morning. And in the afternoon? In a city of 300,000, we went with 250,000 to see a sight no one ever believed was possible. Coventry City's team was on an open-top bus, bringing home the FA Cup. City had been a joke. On 15 December 1970, the satirical 'Monty Python's Flying Circus' had a sketch entitled 'Communist Quiz (World Forum)', featuring its members pretending to be famous Communist leaders from days gone by, one of whom, Che Guevara, was asked, 'Coventry City last won the FA Cup in what year?' Not only did Che look dumbfounded, none of the other contestants could answer either. Eric Idle, the quiz presenter, then told them: 'I'm not surprised you didn't get that. It was in fact a trick question. Coventry City has never won the FA Cup.'

Tottenham Hotspur was bound to win in 1987, even though City had reached the final, to everyone's amazement. By the time the Spurs had gone 2-1 ahead, all seemed lost. From the Sky Blue end of Wembley, the song rang out, echoed in homes in the entire Coventry area:

Go for it
Go for it City
Sky Blues – shooting to win.[5]

Whereupon Keith Houtchen hurled himself forward to head the equalizer, Spurs defender Gary Mabbutt deflected a cross from Coventry's winger Lloyd McGrath into his own net, and Coventry's injured captain Brian Kilcline limped up the steps to the Royal Box to lift the iconic trophy. No wonder almost everyone lined the streets that Sunday afternoon. Coventry City may now languish in the lower divisions of England's Football League, but they, and we, will always have 1987 as the year they won.

We have this one life given to us. Whatever we do, however impossible it may seem, we can 'go for it'. We can be the winners, limping perhaps, to receive the trophy and the 'Well done!' We can be 'finishing well' with our 'faith in later years'. Let's go for it!

And if we have got this far and your pessimism is rearing its ugly head, I have a final exercise for you. The Anglican Church of Kenya, where I was ordained, has written a beautiful new set of services, including a reshaped Communion Service. When this particular liturgy draws to a close, the congregation is invited to stand, and the service leader positions himself in front of the cross and says in a loud voice, 'All our problems', whereupon the entire church sweep their hands from themselves towards the front with the shout, 'we send to the cross of Christ.' It is moving, dramatic and releasing. Pessimists see problems, the 'glass half empty' syndrome. We need to hear again from Isaiah 53.4, 'Surely he took up our infirmities and carried our sorrows.' Peter is right: 'Cast all your anxiety on him because he cares for you' (1 Peter 5.7). Send your problems to the cross of Christ.

The Kenyan service goes on to the next sweep of the hand; in response to the minister's words 'All our difficulties', our shout again is to send these to the cross of Christ. Problems are often from the past, while difficulties lie ahead. How will we survive our bodies' and minds' deterioration, the absence of a partner, the distance of families (the list could be long here)? A difficult future?

Maybe. We need to take in again these wonderful words from Hebrews 13.5–6:

> God has said, 'Never will I leave you; never will I forsake you'. So we say with confidence, 'The Lord is my helper; I will not be afraid. What can man do to me'?

Having dealt with past and future by sending them to the cross of Christ, I am always glad for a third sweep of the hand, as the minister calls out, 'All the devil's works', which we also send to the cross. When I look inside myself, I echo Paul's words, 'When I want to do good, evil is right there with me' (Romans 7.21). Then it is back to Isaiah 53 again, to verses five and six:

> He was pierced for our transgressions, he was crushed for our iniquities; the punishment that brought us peace was upon him, and by his wounds we are healed. We all, like sheep, have gone astray, each of us has turned to his own way; and the Lord has laid on him the iniquity of us all.

Thank God for the cross! Down with the devil; send all his works to the cross. And still there is one final thing to say, but this time, in the Kenyan liturgy, a different hand sweep, this final one being straight upwards. The leader calls out, 'All our hopes', and the congregation raises their hands in the air as we say, 'We set on the Risen Christ.' We are not going nowhere, we are heaven-bound. Jesus will take us there.

'Christ is Risen!' is the triumphal Easter morning greeting, to which we reply, 'He is risen indeed, Allelujah!'

> I know who holds the future
> And he'll guide me with his hand.[6]

References

1 'The best'

1 Browning, R,. 'Rabbi ben Ezra'. 1963. Poems and Plays Vol 2. Everyman's Library, p. 481

2 Tournier, P,. 'Learning to Grow Old'. 1985. Highland Books, p 1-2

3 Gratton, L. and Scott, A., 'The 100-Year Life'. 2017. Bloomsbury Business, p. 19

2 'I'm glad I'm not young . . .'

1 'Gigi' [film] MGM 1958, based on the novella 'Gigi', Colette, 1944.

2 Procol Harum, 'A Whiter Shade of Pale' Derham Records, 1967

3 Gratton, L,. And Scott, A., 'The 100-Year Life', 2017. Bloomsbury Business, p. xii

4 de Saint-Exupéry, A., 'Wind, Sand and Stars', from 'Terre des Hommes'. 1939, 1971. Penguin Modern Classics, p. 181-183

5 Hawn, M.C., (1835-1889) 'Breathe on me Breath of God', Hymn.

6 Springfield, D., 'I Just don't Know What to do with Myself' from the album 'Dusty'. Words and music Burt Bacharach and Hal David, Phillips Label, 1964

7 Dylan, R., 'The Times They are a-Changin', CBS label, 1963.

8 'Big' [film], starring Tom Hanks. Twentieth Century Fox, 1988

9 Shakespeare, W., Cleopatra from 'Anthony and Cleopatra', Act 1 scene 5 l.73

10 Morse, L., 'What's Age Got to Do With It?' 2017. Monarch Books, p. 121

11 Ford, R., 'Let Me Be Frank with You', 2015. Bloomsbury Publishing, p. 34

12 Gratton, L., And Scott, A., 'The 100-Year Life', 2017. Bloomsbury Business, p. 2

13 Gratton, L., And Scott, A., op. cit., p. 3,

14 Williams, W., 'Guide me O Thou great Jehovah', from the Welsh 'Arglwdd, arwain trwy'r anialwch' 1745, translated by Peter Williams 1771

15 Wesley, C., 'And Can it Be' Hymn. 1738

16 The Times Newspaper, 19 August 2017

17 Morse, L., and Hitchings, R., 'Could it be Dementia' 2008. Monarch Books, p. 51

18 Lyte, H.F., 'Abide With Me' 1847

3 Will you still need me?

1 Knox, I., 'Bereaved' 1994. Kingsway p. 30

2 Shakespeare, W., 'Sonnet No 2'. c.1600

3 Ashford, D., 'The Young Visitors', 1919. Zodiac Books

4 Gawande, A., 'Being Mortal' 2015. Profile Books p. 9

5 Nouwen, H., 'Our Greatest Gift' 1995. Harper One p. 13

6 Gilbert, W.S. and Sullivan, A., 'So Please you Sir' The Mikado 1885

7 Ed. Lingiardi, V., and McWilliams, N., 'Psychodynamic Diagnostic Manual' : Second Edition PDM2, 2017. Guildford Press

8 'Life begins at 50: A Better Society for Older People', 2000. Department of Social Security Inter-Ministerial Group for Older People', Foreword

9 Morse, L., 'What's Age Got to Do With It?' 2017. Monarch Books, p. 13

10 Knox, I.S., 'Older People and the Church' 2002. T and T Clark for Continuum p. 16-17,

11 Katz, R.L., 'Jewish Values of Sociopsychological Perspectives on Aging', in 'Towards a Theology of Aging: Pastoral Psychology Special Issue', 1975. Henman Sciences Press, New York p. 135-150

12 Lennon, J. and McCartney, P., 'When I'm 64' from 'Sgt Pepper's Lonely Hearts Club Band', Northern Songs Ltd., 1967

13 Nouwen, H., op. cit., p. 1

14 Taylor, R., 'Three Score Years - and Then?' 2004. Monarch Books p 13

15 Taylor, R., op. cit., p. 14

16 Morse, L., op. cit., p. 96

17 Merchant, R., 'Pioneering the Third Age' 2017. CARE, p. 27

18 'Arthur' film starring Dudley Moore as Arthur and Sir John Gielgood as Hobson, Warner Bros., 1981

19 Tournier, P., 'Learning to Grow Old' 1972. Highland Books p. 2-3

20 Mid 2016 Population Estimates, U.K. Office for National Statistics 2017 (O.N.S.)

21 Mid 2016 Population Estimates, op. cit.

22 Mid 2016 Population Estimates, op. cit.

23 U.K. O.N.S. 2016

24 U.K. O.N.S. 2016

25 National Population Projections for the U.K. 2014, based on the O.N.S. 2015

26 National Population Projections for the U.K. 2014, op. cit.

27 National Population Projections for the U.K. 2014, op. cit.

28 National Population Projections for the U.K. 2014, op. cit.

29 National Population Projections for the U.K. 2014, op. cit.

30 Population Aging in the United Kingdom, its Constituent Countries and the European Union, O.N.S. 2012

31 Labour Forces Survey O.N.S. 2016

32 Labour Forces Survey O.N.S. 2016

33 'Number of Future Centenarians by Age Group': Department of Work and Pensions, 2011

4 'Darling, I am growing old'

1 Shakespeare, W., 'Macbeth' Act 5 Scene 5 lines 19-28

2 Augustine (354-430) Exposition of Psalm 132 from 'A Sermon to the Common People'

3 Dunn, C., 'Grandad', song Flowers, H., and Pickett, K., EMI Columbia, 1970

4 Scrutton, S., in McEwen E., ed. 'Age: The Unrecognised Discrimination', 1990. Age Concern p. 13-14

5 Butler, R.N., 'Age-ism: Another form of Bigotry', 1969. in The Gerontologist 9 (4) p. 243-246,

6 Johnson, J., and Bytheway, B., in Johnson, J., and Slater, R., eds. Ageing and Later Life, 1993. Sage

7 Franklin, A., and Franklin, B., 'Age and Power', in Jeffs and Smith, eds. 'Youth, Inequality and Society', 1990. Macmillan

8 Morse, L., and Hitchings, R., 'Living Out God's Purpose in our Senior Years', 1990. Pilgrims' Friend Society p. 4

9 Morse, L., 'What's Age Got to Do With It?' 2017. Monarch Books p. 17

10 Kitwood, T., 'Dementia Reconsidered' 1997. Open University Press p. 12

11 Yeats, W.B., 'Sailing to Byzantium' v 2, 1928 in W.B. Yeats Sailing to Byzantium 1995. Phoenix

12 Binyon, R.L., 'For the Fallen' v4, first published The Times
    21 September 1914

13 Coleman, P., Bond, J., and Peace, S., 'Ageing in the Twentieth
    Century' in Coleman, P., Bond, J., and Peace, S., Eds. 'Ageing in
    Society' 1993. Sage p. 1-18

14 Eds. Lingiardi, V., and McWilliams, N., PDM-2 2017

15 Rippon, I., et al, 'Perceived Age Discrimination in Older Adults'
    in 'Age and Ageing' Vol 3. Issue 3, p. 379-386 May 2014

16 Rippon, I., op. cit. p. 379-386

17 'One voice: Shaping our Ageing Society', 2009. Age Concern and
    Help the Aged

18 'One voice' op. cit.

19 Merchant, R., 'Pioneering the Third Age' 2017 Care . p. 11

20 Nouwen, H.J., and Gaffney, W.J., 'Aging: The Fulfilment of Life'
    1976. Image Doubleday p. 17

21 de Beauvoir, S., 'The Coming of Age' 1972. Putman p. 550

22 Howe, A., 'Attitudes to Ageing: Views of Older People and the
    Community' in St. Mark's Review 155 (Spring) 1993. p. 3-11

23 Laslett, P., 'A Fresh Map of Life: The Emergence of the Third Age'
    1989. Weidenfield and Nicolson p. 1

24 Gawande, A., 'Being Mortal' 2015. Profile p. 14

25 PDM-2 op. cit.

26 Gratton, L., and Scott, A., 'The 100-Year Life' 2017. Bloomsbury
    Business p. 322-3

27 Tournier, P., 'Learning to Grow Old' 1972. SCM p. 37

28 Watson, S., 'Pasta, parkas, polyamory: the new you in 2018'
    Times 2, The Times, 1 January 2018

29 Knox, I.S., 'Older People and the Church' 2002. T and T Clark
    for Continuum p. 64-83

30 Knox, I.S., op. cit. at p. 65

31 Taylor, R., 'Wake up to old age!' 1996. Anglicans for Renewal Magazine 67, p. 13-14,

32 Taylor, R. op. cit.

33 Creber, A., 'Evangelism among Retired People' 1994. Church Pastoral Aid Society p. 5

34 Gray, R.M. and Moberg, D.O. 'The Church and the Older Person' 1962. Eerdmans p. 19-36

35 Merchant, R., op. cit. at p. 10-11

36 Rexford, E.E., 'Silver Threads Among the Gold' song, 1873

37 Townshend,P., 'My Generation' song, The Who, Brunswick Label, October 1965

38 Smith, P., 'Old Age is Another Country' 1995. Crossing Press

39 Ford, R., 'Let Me be Frank with You' 2015. Bloomsbury Paperbacks p. 160

40 Thomas, M., 'The Curse of Older Age' 1999. Plus 15 (3) p. 10-11

41 Swift, J., 'Thoughts on Various Subjects' 1727

42 Jung, C.G. 'Modern Man in Search of a Soul' 1933 Routledge

43 Tournier, P. op. cit. p. 12

44 Tournier, P. op. cit. p. 185

45 Prime, D., 'A Good Old Age' 2017. 10 Publishing p. 4, 11-16

46 Roth, P., 'Everyman' 2007. Vintage p. 156

47 Roth, P., op. cit. p. 143-144

48 Tournier, P. op. cit. p. 187

49 McCrum, R., 'Every Third Thought' 2017. Picador p. 7

50 McCrum, R., op. cit. p. 9

51 Cryer, B., quoted in Benson, R., 'Old Git Wit' 2006. Summersdale

52 Gawande, A., op. cit. p. 55

53 Gawande, A., op. cit. p. 146-147

54 Springfield, D., 'I just don't know what to do with myself' op. cit.

55 Simon, P., from 'America' song v 5, in 'Bookends', Simon and Garfunkel, Columbia Records, 1968

56 Smith, S., 'Not Waving but Drowning' Poem, in 'The Nation's Favourite Poems' 1996 BBC p. 16

57 U.K. Poverty 2017, Report by the Joseph Rowntree Foundation, Dec 2017

58 Queen Elizabeth, the Queen Mother (1900-2002) quoted in 'Old Git Wit' op. cit. p. 52

59 McCrum, R., op. cit. p. 23

60 McCrum, R., op. cit. p. 220-221

61 Lewis, C.S. izquotes.com

5 Heroes and zeros

1 Carre, E.G., 'Praying Hyde: A Challenge to Prayer', 1983. Bridge-Logos

2 Merchant, R., 'Pioneering the Third Age', 2017. CARE p. 44

3 Merchant, R., op. cit. p. 63

4 Knox, I.S., 'Older People and the Church', 2002. T and T Clark for Continuum p. 142

5 Gill, J., 'Exposition of the old Testament – 2 Samuel' 1747-63

6 Marley, G.T., 'Hushai' in Douglas, J.D. ed 'The New Bible Dictionary', 1962. Inter-Varsity Fellowship p. 548

7 Merchant, R., op. cit. p. 47

8 Knox, I.S., op. cit. p. 140

9 Carmichael, A., quoted in

10 Lattimore, 'Acts and Letters of the Apostles', 1982. Farrar Straus Giroux p. 26

11 Gooding, D., 'True to the Faith', 1990. Hodder and Stoughton p. 55

12 Merchant, R., op. cit. p. 48

13 Wyatt, J., 'Matters of Life and Death' 2009. Inter-Varsity Press p. 73

14 Wyatt, J., op. cit. p. 74

15 Thompson, J., 'Jeremiah' in 'The New Bible Dictionary', Ed. Douglas, J.D., 1962. Inter-Varsity Fellowship p. 608

16 Knox, I.S., op. cit. p. 143

17 Kidner, D., 'Genesis' Tyndale Old Testament Commentaries, 1967. Inter-Varsity Press p. 103

18 Payne, D.F., 'Genesis, Exodus', 1970. Scripture Union p. 12

19 Sinatra, F., 'I Did it My Way', lyrics Paul Anka, Reprise Records label, 1969

20 Wesley, J., Journal 28 June, 1783

6 To be or . . .

1 Shakespeare, W., 'Hamlet' Act 3 Scene 1 lines 57-61. 1599-1602

2 Descartes, R., 'Discourse on the Method' 1637

3 Waters, R., 'Smell the Roses' from Album 'Is This the Life We Really Want?' track 9, 2 June 2017, Colombia label

4 Sears, E.H., 'It Came upon the Midnight Clear' Carol 1849

5 Weber, M., 'The Protestant Ethic and the Spirit of Capitalism' 1905 Transl. Parsons, Talcot, 2003. Dover

6 Gooding, D., 'An Unshakeable Kingdom', 1989 . IVP p. 121-123

7 The Times 3.1.18

8 Brother Lawrence, 'The Practice of the Presence of God' 1693

9 Brother Lawrence, Wikipedia 2017

10 Roth, P., 'Everyman' 2007. Vintage p. 102

11 Prime, D., 'A Good Old Age' 2017. 10 Publishing p. 61-67

12 Wright, T., 'Revelation for Everyone' 2011. SPCK

13 Wright, T., 'For everyone: Bible Study Guides – Revelation. 2012. SPCK

14 Graham, B., 'Nearing Home' 2011. Thomas Nelson p. 44

15 Eds. Lingiardi, V., and McWilliams, N., PDM2 2017. Guildford Press

16 Graham, B., op. cit. p. 50

17 Prime, D., op. cit. p. 49

18 Tournier, P., 'Learning to Grow Old' 1972. SCM p. 43

19 Graham, B., op. cit. vii

20 Graham, B., op. cit. p. 106-108

21 Graham, B., op. cit. p. 43

22 Pond, C., 'Autumn Gold', 2001. Grace Publications Trust p. 41-42

7 Not retired – refired!

1 de Saint-Exupéry, A., 'Wind, Sand and Stars', from 'Terre des Hommes'. 1939, Penguin Modern Classics 1971 at p. 181-183

2 Packer, J.I., 'Finishing our Course with Joy' 2014. IVP p. 18, 22

3 Tournier, P., 'Learning to Grow Old' 1972. SCM p. 20-21

4 Gratton, L., and Scott, A., 'The 100-Year Life', 2017. Bloomsbury Business, p. xiii

5 Tournier, P., op. cit. (quoting Jung, C.G., 'Modern Man in Search of a Soul' 1933. Routledge p11

6 Graham, B., 'Nearing Home' 2011. Thomas Nelson p. ix

7 Bridge, M., The Times, 22 January 2018. p. 4

8 Smyth, C., The Times op. cit. p. 4

9 Morse, L., 'What's Age Got to Do With It?' 2017. Monarch Books

10 Packer, J.I., op. cit. p. 50

11 McCrum, R., 'Every Third Thought' 2017. Picador p. 150

12 Sparrow, J., 1906-92

13 Eds. Lingiardi, V., and McWilliams, N., PDM2 2017. Guildford Press

14 Gratton, L., and Scott, A., op. cit. p. 266

15 Gratton, L,. and Scott, A,. op. cit. p. 195

16 Marr, A., 'A History of Modern Britain' 2007. Macmillan

17 Gratton, L,. and Scott, A,. op. cit. p. 273-274

18 Knox, I.S., 'Older People and the Church', 2002. T and T Clark for Continuum p. 183-210

19 Matheson, J., and Summerfield, C., eds. 'Social Focus on Older People' 1999. The Stationery Office p. 7

20 Packer, J.I., op. cit. p. 64

21 Merchant, R., 'Pioneering the Third Age', 2017. CARE p. 14

22 Packer, J.I., op. cit. p. 92-93

23 Winter, R., 'The Retirement Booby Trap' Mission Frontiers 7 July 1985. p. 25 in Piper, J., 'Desiring God' 1986. IVP p. 187

24 Piper, J., op. cit. p. 187

25 Winchester Baptist Church:

26 Osborn, A., 'Let the Beauty of Jesus' chorus 1947

27 Tournier, P., op. cit. p. 68

28 Pond, A., 'Autumn Gold' 2001. Grace Publications p. 59

8 Can't teach an old dog?

1 Wold, S.G., 'You Can't Teach an Old Dog New Tricks', Reprise Records label, 1969

2 Hudson Pope, R., CSSM Choruses No. 1 1936. CSSM no. 298

3 Carroll, L., 'Advice from a Caterpillar' from 'Alice's Adventures in Wonderland', 1865. Chapter 5

4 Aladdin, from 'One Thousand and One Nights', in 'Arabian Nights', 1706. (English Translation)

5 Knox, I., 'Bereaved' 1994, 2003. Kingsway p. 48-50

6 Packer, J.I., 'Finishing our Course with Joy' 2014. IVP p. 25-26

7 Graham, B., 'Nearing Home' 2011. Thomas Nelson p. 138

8 McCrum, R., 'Every Third Thought' 2017. Picador p. 203-4

9 Share it!

1 Mercer, J., and Arlen, H., (lyricists) 'Accentuate the Positive'. Bing Crosby and the Andrews Sisters (et al.) Decca label, 1944

2 Knox. I., 'Fifty Ways to Share Your Faith', 2002. Kingsway

3 Merchant, R., 'Pioneering the Third Age', 2017. CARE p. 135

4 Packer, J.I., 'Finishing our Course with Joy' 2014. IVP p. 84

5 Taylor, R., 'Three Score Years - and Then?' 2001. Monarch Books p. 25

6 Taylor, R., op. cit. p. 27

7 Reaching Out to the Elderly. London City Mission , <lcm.org.uk> N.D.

8 Stacey, E., 'How to Run a Holiday at Home for Seniors' <liz@winbap .org.uk>

9 Pilgrims' Friend Society, 'Sharing the Good News of Jesus' 2017. PFS <info@pilgrimsfriend.org.uk>

10 Words: Will H. Houghton (c) 1936, Ren. 1964 Hope Publishing Company, Carol Stream IL 60188. All rights reserved. Used by permission.

10 Hang on in there

1 Bristol, J., 'Hang on in There, Baby' song, MGM, 1974

2 Barlow, G., 'Hang on in There, Baby' song, MGM, 1988

3 Sacks, J., 'Surviving Crisis' 2009. in Covenant and Conversation, Maggid Books and The Orthodox Union p. 229-233

4 James, W., 'A Pluralistic Universe' (quotation 1900) 2011. The Floating Press

5 Mendelssohn, F., 'He that shall endure', from 'Elijah' 1846. Op. 70, No. 32

6 Wesley, C., 'Love Divine' 1747. Hymn (last verse)

11 Feel the fog

1 Gibbon, M., (1737-1794), 'The Decline and Fall of the Roman Empire' (abridged Low D.M.), 1972, Book Club Associates)

2 Browning, R., 'Prospice' in 'Poems and Plays', Vol 2. 1963. Everyman's Library p. 512

3 Clifford, A., 'Time to Live' 2017. Instant Apostle p. 21

4 Clifford, A., op. cit. p. 41

5 Gawande, A., 'Being Mortal' 2015. Profile p. 8

6 McCrum, R., 'Every Third Thought' 2017. Picador p. 206

7 Shakespeare, W., 'The Tempest' Act 5, Sc 1 L327

8 Wyatt, J., 'Matters of Life and Death' 2009. Inter-Varsity Press p 191

9 Levine, S., 'Who dies?' 1986. Gateway p. 1

10 Nouwen, H., 'Our Greatest Gift' 1995. Harper One p. xiv

11 Allen, W., <www.brainyquote.com>

12 Thiele, B., and Weiss, G.D. 'Cabaret' song, Louis Armstrong. ABC label, 1967

13 Nouwen, H., op. cit. p. 3

14 McCrum, R., op. cit. p. 6

15 Nouwen, H., op. cit. p. 16

16 Tournier, P., 'Learning to Grow Old' 1972. SCM p. 222-223

17 Gratton, L,. and Scott, A,. 'The 100-Year Life', 2017. Bloomsbury Business, p. 329

18 Clifford, A., op. cit. p. 83

19 Wyatt, J., op. cit. p. 191-214

20 Eds. Lingiardi, V., and McWilliams, N., PDM-2 2017 Guildford Press

21 Levine, S., op. cit. p. 73

22 Clifford, A., op. cit. p. 13-216

23 Knox, I., 'Bereaved' 2003. Kingsway

24 Graham, B., 'Nearing Home' 2011. Thomas Nelson p. viii

25 McCrum, R., op. cit. p. 155

26 Barnes, J., 'Levels of Life' 2014. Vintage p. 78

27 Barnes, J., op. cit. p. 94

28 Morse, L., 'Dementia: Frank and Linda's Story' 2010. Monarch p. 8

29 Tournier, P., op. cit. p. 16

30 Wyatt, J., op. cit. p. 228

31 Clifford, A., op. cit. p79

32 Levine, S., op. cit. p. 290

33 Morse, L., op. cit. p. 119

34 Graham, B., op. cit. p. 166-7

35 Prime, D., 'A Good Old Age' 2017. 10 Publishing p. 58

36 McElhinney, L., 'Faith and Hope in the Midst of Motor Neurone Disease', You Tube 15th January 2016

37 McElhinney, L., 'Solid Joys and Lasting Treasures' <www.simply orderit.com/mnd> (permission granted)

12 The long goodbye

1 Clift, E., and Thomas, E., Newsweek, 21 June 2004

2 Dunham, W., Reuters, in Christian Science Monitor, 6 March 2016

3 Johnson, K., 'The Long Goodbye' 2011. Apple Music

4 Gratton, L,. and Scott, A,. 'The 100-Year Life', 2017. Bloomsbury Business, p. 37

5 Gawande, A., 'Being Mortal' 2015. Profile p. 31

6 James, O., 'Contented Dementia' 2009. Vermillion p. 7

7 Swinton, J., 'Dementia: Living in the Memories of God' 2017. SCM p. 187

8 Swinton, J., op. cit. p. 187

9 Morse, L., and Hitchings, R., 'Could it be Dementia?' 2008. Monarch p. 154-155

10 Knox, I.S., 'Older People and the Church', 2002. T and T Clark for Continuum p. 249

11 James, O., op. cit. p. 7

12 Morse, L., and Hitchings, R., op. cit. p. 13

13 Kitwood, T., 'Dementia Reconsidered' 1997. Open University Press p. 21

14 Kitwood, T., op. cit. p. 20-36

15 Kitwood, T., op. cit. p. 136

16 Swinton, J., op. cit. p. 107-108

17 Swinton, J., op. cit. p. 58

18 McCrum, R., 'Every Third Thought' 2017. Picador p. 66

19 Morse, L., 'Dementia: Frank and Linda's Story' 2010. Monarch p 36-37

20 Stokes, G., 'And Still the Music Plays' 2009. Hawker p. 62

21 Swinton, J., op. cit. p. 157

22 Stokes, G., op. cit. p. 21

23 Saunders, J., 'Dementia: Pastoral Theology and Pastoral Care' 2002. Grove in Merchant , R., 'Pioneering the Third Age' 2017 CARE p. 19

24 Swinton, J., op. cit. p. 56

25 Mulligan, C., 'Dementia is not a natural part of getting old' The Times. 11 Dec 2017 p. 30

26 Stokes, G., op. cit. p. 101

27 Smyth, C., 'Dementia will Overwhelm Healthcare' The Times. 8 Dec 2017 p. 2

28 Petzsch, H.M.J., 'Does he Know how Frightening he is in his Strangeness? A study of Attitudes to Dementing People' 1984. Centre for Theology and Public Issues

29 Swinton, J., op. cit. p. 1-2

30 Kitwood, T., op. cit. p. 82

31 Malvern, J., 'Tourist Sites told to become Dementia Friendly or Lose Income' The Times. 1 January 2018

32 The Times, Leader, 'Illness and Independence' 28 Dec 2017 p. 35

33 Elliott, V., 'Garden where memories grow' The Times 1 June 1999 p. 9

34 James, O., op. cit. p. 220-221

35 Stokes, G., op. cit. p. 184

36 'Suggestions for visiting people with dementia' <www.glorious opportunity.org> and 'Contented Dementia' Trust

37 Kitwood, T., op. cit. p. 7

38 Bonhoeffer, D., 'Who am I?' in 'Letters and Papers from Prison, ed. And translated Fuller, R., 1959 repr 1963 Fontana Books p. 173

39 Morse, L., 'Frank and Linda' op. cit. p. 35

40 Wyatt, J., 'Matters of Life and Death' 2009. IVP p. 235

41 Wyatt, J., op. cit. p. 60-61

42 Swinton, J., op. cit. p. 20

43 Swinton, J., op. cit. p. 157

44 Swinton, J., op. cit. p. 160

45 Swinton, J., op. cit. p. 165

46 Stokes, G., op. cit. p. 217

47 Barnes, P., 'On the Edge of Ministry' Australian Presbyterian Magazine, in Evangelical Times October 2010

48 Graham, B., 'Nearing Home' 2011. Thomas Nelson p. 85

49 Treetops, J., 'A Daisy among the Dandelions', 1992. Faith in Elderly People (Leeds) p. 6

13 Who cares?

1 Carers Trust, <https://carers.org>

2 Nouwen, H., 'Our Greatest Gift' 1995. Harper One p. 14

3 Graham, B., 'Nearing Home' 2011. Thomas Nelson p. 48

4 Wyatt, J., 'Matters of Life and Death' 2009. IVP p. 65

5 Knox, I., 'Bereaved' 2003. Kingsway p. 272

6 Wise, G., 'Not that Kind of Love' Quercus, 2018, in The Times Magazine, 10 Feb 2018 p. 22-29

7 Morse, L., and Hitchings, R., 'Could it be Dementia?' 2008. Monarch p. 152-153

8 Knox, I., op. cit. p. 238-239

9 Buchanan, A., 'Letters to the Editor', The Times 22 Nov 2017 p 30

10 Ward, C., 'Growing up in Kinship Care' Report by Grandparents Plus 29 Nov 2017

11 Wyatt, J., op. cit. p. 76

12 Roth, R., 'Let me be Frank with You' 2015. Bloomsbury p. 140

13 Morse, L., and Hitchings, R., op. cit. p. 187-189

14 Nouwen, H., op. cit. p. 55-56, 87, 96

15 Keats, J., 'Ode to a Nightingale' 1819. lines 24-25

16 National End of Life Care Intelligence Network 'Death of Older Adults in England October 2010

17 Morse, L., and Hitchings, R., op. cit. p. 153-154

18 Hurst, G., 'Shared joy of care that brings young and old together' The Times 18 Nov 2017 p. 24

19 Hurst, G., 'Build care homes by schools to mix generations' The Times 5 Jan 2018 p. 24

20 Paterson, L., 'Terminally ill 'not cared for properly'' The Times (Scottish Edition) 6 Feb 2018 p. 13

21 Paterson, L., op. cit.

22 Srivsatava, R., 'Chasing deadlines and happiness, we forget our lonely elderly' The Guardian 12 Oct 2017

23 'Reaching out to the Elderly' London City Mission p. 5, <lcm.org.uk>

24 Nouwen, H., op. cit. p. 59

25 James, O., 'Contented dementia' 2008. Vermillion p. 200

26 James, O., op. cit. p. 209

27 James, O., op. cit. p. 211-212

28 Kitwood, T., 'Dementia Reconsidered' 1997. Open University Press p. 109-112

29 Wyatt, J., op. cit. p. 220

30 Morse, L., 'Dementia: Frank and Linda's Story' 2010. Monarch p. 92

31 Wyatt, J., op. cit. p. 235

32 Morse, L., and Hitchings, R., op. cit. p. 123

33 Edwards, J., in Piper, J., 'Desiring God' 1986. IVP p. 88

34 Knox, I., op. cit. p. 247

14 Go for it

1 Aesop. 'Fables' 6th Century BC

2 Jarvis, M. and Powell, C., 'Uncle Bob Builds a Boat' 2017. Books Direct; Neilson/Amazon

3 Lemmel, H.H., 'O soul are you weary and troubled?' Hymn 1922

4 Adkins, G.R., 'By and by' Hymn 1948

5 Taylor, S., and Taylor, H., 'Go for it!' Song 1987 on 'Cov Classics' Cherry Red Label 1998

6 Clarke, E.I. and Smith, A.B., 'I know who holds the future' Hymn (ND)

Faith in later life

There are 11.9 million people over the age of 65 in the UK[1], with an increasing number of churches reporting a rise in the number of their older members. Older people are to be valued, according to the Scriptures, (Leviticus 19:32) and we are told that older believers will flourish and still bear fruit in old age (Psalm 92:12-14).

On a mission to encourage Christians and churches to reach, serve and empower older people, **Faith in Later Life** was established in 2017 by a group of Christian charities (Pilgrims' Friend Society, The Salvation Army, London City Mission, Keychange, and Mission Care) that have been engaging with older people for hundreds of years.

With older people often marginalised by society, but Church naturally intergenerational by design, **Faith in Later Life** seeks to shine a light on the gifts and wisdom that older Christians have, often built up over a lifetime of following Jesus, and to encourage churches to make the most of their senior members, and affirm their older believers in their identify in Christ, that they may know that God has plans for His people, whatever their age. And as Christians reach out to older people in their wider community, we desire to see many older people come to know Jesus Christ as their Lord and Saviour.

---

1. Age UK research, May 2019

Faith in Later Life seeks to equip Christians and churches through its website, as well as an international network of Church Champions; and provides an online resource hub of over 150 books and articles, each relating to different aspects of later life.

You can find out more about Faith in Later Life at <www.faithinlaterlife.org>

Carl Knightly
Chief Executive, Faith in Later Life

WE HAVE A VISION OF A WORLD IN WHICH EVERYONE IS TRANSFORMED BY CHRISTIAN KNOWLEDGE

As well as being an award-winning publisher, SPCK is the oldest Anglican mission agency in the world.

Our mission is to lead the way in creating books and resources that help everyone to make sense of faith.

Will you partner with us to put good books into the hands of prisoners, great assemblies in front of schoolchildren and reach out to people who have not yet been touched by the Christian faith?

To donate, please visit www.spckpublishing.co.uk/donate or call our friendly fundraising team on 020 7592 3900.

An easy way to get to know the Bible

'For those who've been putting aside two years in later life to read the Bible from cover to cover, the good news is: the most important bits are here.' Jeremy Vine, BBC Radio 2

The Bible is full of dramatic stories that have made it the world's bestselling book. But whoever has time to read it all from cover to cover? Now here's a way of getting to know the Bible without having to read every chapter and verse.

No summary, no paraphrase, no commentary: just the Bible's own story in the Bible's own words.

'What an amazing concept! This compelling, concise, slimmed-down Scripture is a must for anyone who finds those sixty-six books a tad daunting.'
Paul Kerensa, comedian and script writer

'A great introduction to the main stories in the Bible and it helps you to see how they fit together. It would be great to give as a gift.'

Five-star review on Amazon

The One Hour Bible
978 0 281 07964 3 • £4.99